W9-BIP-105

GREAT AMERICAN QUILTS

BOOK NINE

Edited by
Patricia Wilens

Great American Quilts Book Nine

©2001 by Oxmoor House, Inc.
Book Division of Southern Progress Corporation
P.O. Box 2463, Birmingham, Alabama 35201

Published by Oxmoor House, Inc., and Leisure Arts, Inc.

All rights reserved. No part of this book may be reproduced in any form or by any means without the prior written permission of the publisher, excepting brief quotations in connection with reviews written specifically for inclusion in magazines or newspapers, or single copies for strictly personal use.

We're Here for You!
We at Oxmoor House are dedicated to serving you with reliable information that expands your imagination and enriches your life. We welcome your comments and suggestions. Please write us at:

> Oxmoor House, Inc.
> Editor, *Great American Quilts*
> 2100 Lakeshore Drive
> Birmingham, AL 35209

To order additional publications, call 800-633-4910.

ISBN: 0-8487-2447-x
ISSN: 0890-8222
Printed in the United States of America
First Printing 2001

Editor-in-Chief: Nancy Fitzpatrick Wyatt
Senior Crafts Editor: Susan Ramey Cleveland
Senior Editor, Copy and Homes: Olivia K. Wells
Art Director: Cynthia R. Cooper

Editor: Patricia Wilens
Contributing Copy Editor: Susan S. Cheatham
Contributing Designer: Barbara Ball
Illustrator: Kelly Davis
Senior Photographers: Jim Bathie, John O'Hagan
Photographer: Brit Huckabay
Contributing Photographer: Keith Harrelson
Senior Photo Stylist: Kay Clarke
Contributing Stylists: Melanie Clarke, Cathy Harris
Publishing Systems Administrator: Rick Tucker
Director, Production and Distribution: Phillip Lee
Book Production Manager: Theresa L. Beste
Production Assistant: Faye Porter Bonner

For more books to enrich your life, visit **oxmoorhouse.com**

Great American Quilts come from every region of the United States. This year's book features quilters from 20 states. If your state isn't represented, perhaps you can make a mark on next year's map. To submit a quilt for consideration, just send a snapshot with your name, address, and phone number to *Great American Quilts*, Oxmoor House, 2100 Lakeshore Drive, Birmingham, AL 35209. Deadline for the 2003 edition is December 31, 2001. We cannot return photos.

Welcome to *Great American Quilts 2002*

Remember when your birthday present or Christmas gift was that longed-for *big* box of crayons? A child has yet to live who isn't thrilled by the bright box with a sharpener on the back and a rainbow of crayons inside. Is a 64-crayon box better than the 16-pack? You bet it is. Most quiltmakers feel the same way about fabric. We love having lots and *lots* of fabric.

With fabric lovers and collectors in mind, our opening chapter offers quilts that satisfy the need to have and to use as many fabrics as possible. **Crayon Box Scrap Quilts** are bright, muticolored, and cheerful. *Wild Stars* is a classic pattern made "way cool" with splashy fabrics and clever piecing. *Careening & Circling* takes a simple two-patch block into the new millenium with a creative set, while *San Diego Sunset* celebrates the lure of popular batiks.

Quilts Across America showcases appealing designs from coast to coast. Quiet elegance defines *Diana's Rose*. You'll find old-time charm in *Christmas Holly* and *Fleur-de-lis*, as well as striking modern looks in *Lacquer Luster* and *Reflections*.

Classic design, enhanced by new techniques and reproduction fabrics, is the focus of **Traditions in Quilting.** You'll appreciate the grace of *Delectable Mountains*, the sweetness of *Jenny's Flower Garden*, and the folk-art style of *Communion*.

Designer Gallery is a wonderland of innovation and artistry. Enjoy the works of superlative quilt art, such as Jane Blair's exquisitely embroidered *Remembrance*, Robbi Joy Eklow's surrealistic *Half Past Midnight*, and Rebecca Chapin's prizewinning *Garden Cloth*. For a giggle, don't miss Rosellen Carolan's *The Kitty Wampus Family Album*.

Look for the bumblebee illustration that indicates a quilt made by a team, guild, or bee.

Crayon Box Scrap Quilts

Quilts Across America

Quilt Smart

Traditions in Quilting

Designer Gallery

Crayon Box Scrap Quilts

Wild Stars

Relative Comfort

San Diego Sunset

Careening & Circling

Folk Art Flowers & Flies

Megan's Favorite

Jan C. Wildman
Orlando, Florida

*J*an Wildman finished three quilts in the first four years she quilted. "But I bought enough fabric for about 300 quilts!" Jan remembers. Maybe using up that fabric was a motivation when Jan decided to quit her job as an engineer. "I find that being a quilter, wife, and mother is more than a full-time job," she says.

"Being a quilter, wife, and mother is more than a full-time job."

Now Jan finds teaching quilting to be wonderfully rewarding. "Students challenge me to continue to devise ways to obtain better results," she says. "It's delightful when students say that I've changed how they work or that I've opened a new door for them." At the end of a class, seeing her students' finished quilts "is almost as good as finishing one of my own, but without as much work!"

Jan still finds real satisfaction in finishing her own quilts. "I enjoy every aspect of the process," she says. "I truly delight in making quilts."

Wild Stars
2000

A sawtooth star is about as traditional a block as you can get. But Jan Wildman transforms the ordinary with some fabric and a plan.

First, the fabric. It helps to have a mighty stash like Jan's. Some fabrics are big, splashy florals or novelty prints; others are versatile tone-on-tones and textures.

"There is a fabulous variety of fabrics available today," Jan says. "The challenge is to use as much of it as possible."

The easy-to-make star block gets extra jazz from checkerboard sashing and borders.

For the machine quilting, Jan used her own technique that she teaches. The quilted wiggly lines and circles are typical of this method, in which she uses simple, sometimes whimsical, designs in asymmetrical repeats without marking the quilt top. Jan is planning to write a book on her technique.

Wild Stars was shown at the 2000 Houston Quilt Festival's Faculty Showcase.

Wild Stars

Finished Size
Quilt: 77" x 87"
Blocks: 42 (8" x 8")

Materials*
42 (9" x 22") fat eighths light
    print scrap fabrics
42 (9" x 22") fat eighths dark
    print scrap fabrics
1¼ yards white fabric
4¼ yards dark purple border
    fabric (includes binding)
5¼ yards backing fabric
* *Note:* As in all scrap quilts,
these yardages are recommendations. Yardage is sufficient to get
1 star and 1 background from
each fabric. Use your own scraps
and fabric placement as desired.

Cutting
Instructions are for rotary cutting and quick piecing. Cut
pieces in order listed to make
best use of yardage. When possible, pieces are listed in order
needed, so you don't have to cut
everything all at once.

Diagram A

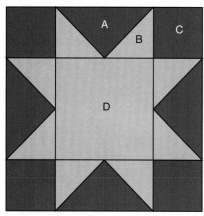

Sawtooth Star Block—Make 42.

From each *scrap fabric*
- 1 (1½" x 22") strip for
    checkerboard border.
- 1 (2½" x 22") strip. From
    this, cut 4 (2½") C squares.
- 1 (4½") D square.
- 4 (2½" x 4½") A pieces.
- 8 (2½") B squares.

From white fabric
- 54 (1½" x 22") strips for
    checkerboard sashing.

From purple fabric
- 4 (5" x 81") lengthwise strips
    for outer border. Use 81"-
    long remnant for next cut.
- 54 (1½" x 22") strips for
    checkerboard sashing.
- 40 (1½" x 22") strips for
    checkerboard border.
- 1 (30") square for binding.

Block Assembly
1. For each block, choose 4 A
pieces and 4 C squares of same
fabric, as well as 8 B squares and
1 D of a coordinating fabric.
2. See Quilt Smart on page 59
for step-by-step instructions for
diagonal-corner quick-piecing
technique. Following those
directions, sew B squares to corners of each A piece as shown
(*Diagram A*). Press.
3. Lay out all units in rows
(*Block Assembly Diagram*). Join
units in each row. Press seam
allowances toward Cs and D.
Join rows to complete block.
4. Make 42 blocks.

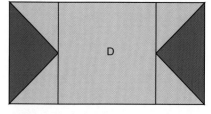

Block Assembly Diagram

Quilt Assembly
1. Using 1½" x 22" strips, join 2
purple and 2 white strips (*Diagram B*). Make 27 strip sets. Press
seam allowances toward purple.
2. Cut 14 (1½"-wide) segments
from each strip set to get a total
of 378 segments.
3. Join 2 segments end-to-end
to make each sashing unit, alternating white and purple fabrics.
Make 84 (8-square) sashing
units. Press joining seam allowances toward purple.
4. Lay out blocks in 7 horizontal
rows with 6 blocks in each row
(*Row Assembly Diagram*). Place
1 sashing unit at both ends of
each row.
5. Join 2 sashing units side-by-
side, turning 1 unit to alternate

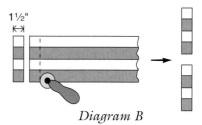

Diagram B

Row Asssembly Diagram—Make 7.

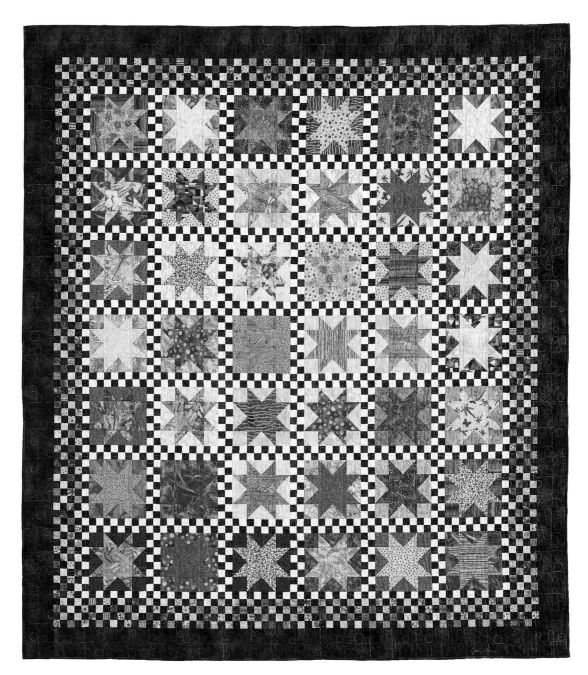

white and purple fabrics *(Row Assembly Diagram)*. Make 35 double-sashing units, 5 for each row. Add double units to layout between blocks in each row.

6. Join blocks and sashing in each row.

7. Referring to photo, join remaining sashing units in 14 horizontal rows with 15 segments in each row. Press joining seam allowances toward purple.

8. Sew 1 sashing row to top edge of first block row and 1 sashing row to bottom edge of last block row, matching seam lines where row meets vertical sashing unit. Press.

9. Referring to photo, join remaining rows in horizontal pairs. Join all rows, alternating sashing rows and block rows.

Borders

1. Make 20 strip sets as before, using 2 (1½" x 22") strips each of purple and assorted scrap fabrics *(Diagram B)*. Press all seam allowances toward purple. You'll have about 40 strips left over; save these for another project.

2. Cut 14 (1½"-wide) segments from each strip set to get a total of 276 (and 4 extra) segments.

3. Referring to photo, join 78 segments side-by-side for each side border, alternating purple and scrap fabrics. Before you press these joining seams, lay each border against quilt edge to determine which border edge aligns so that fabric colors alternate correctly against checkerboard sashing. Mark this inside edge of border with a pin, if desired. Press seam allowances toward segments with a purple square at inside edge.

4. Sew assembled borders to quilt sides.

5. In same manner, join 60 strip-set segments in a row for top border. Identify inside edge and press seam allowances; then sew border to top edge of quilt.

Repeat for bottom border.

6. Measure length of quilt top through middle of pieced section. Trim 2 outer border strips to match quilt length. Sew borders to quilt sides, easing to fit as needed. Press seam allowances toward borders.

7. Measure width of quilt top through middle, including side borders. Trim remaining borders to match width. Sew borders to top and bottom edges of quilt,

easing to fit as needed. Press seam allowances toward borders.

Quilting and Finishing

1. Assemble backing. Layer backing, batting, and quilt top.

2. Quilt as desired. Quilt shown is machine-quilted with an all-over pattern.

3. Make 9½ yards of bias or straight-grain binding from reserved fabric. Bind quilt edges.

Color Variations

Your star quilt can be wild or not so wild in many different ways.
Here are some possibilities to inspire you.

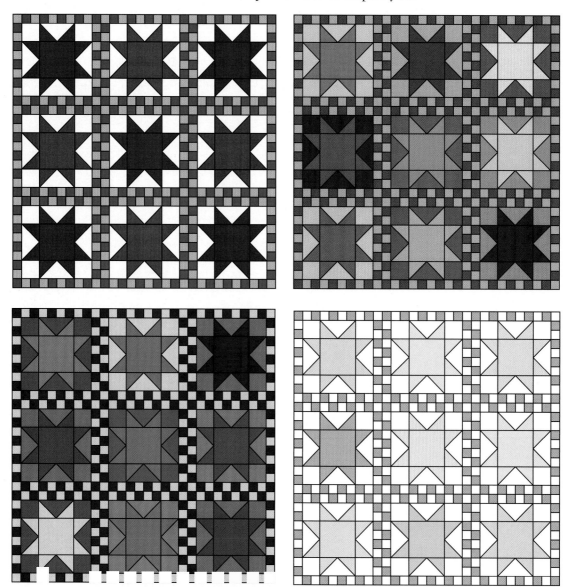

Mary L. Hackett
Carterville, Illinois

Former art teacher Mary Hackett gave up painting when her children were small. When she returned to the studio, she discovered that fabric was more satisfying than watercolors.

"Innovation is the soul of quilt tradition."

A quiltmaker for nearly 15 years, Mary says, "Quilting plays many roles in my life—stress reducer, creative outlet, income source, and treasured skill." She exhibits her work nationally and makes commissioned pieces for private homes and public spaces. "I've been blessed with some success and many sobering rejections," she says. "I find this is a profession that expands and contracts according to how much time and attention I can give it."

Above all, Mary believes in the innovation and creativity that made quilting a strong American art form. "I reject nothing that occurs to me," she says of her work. When she teaches quiltmaking classes, she says, "I enjoy bringing out the creativity that is in everyone."

Mary is a member of Shawnee Quilters of southern Illinois.

Relative Comfort
2000

Mary Hackett believes in doing her own thing, even if that sometimes means defying convention. While she worked on this quilt, Mary was talking with her children about that very subject. "As I stitched," she says, "I thought about how we patch over or ignore flaws to maintain comfort in our lives." She decided to celebrate this quilt's irregularities instead of trying to hide them.

Mary chose pastels for the cross pieces to contrast with the bright squares and triangles. She placed the brights so that each circle blends into the next. She also designed a half-block to avoid cutting off the circles at the quilt's edges.

Mary used high-contrast black thread for hand and machine outline-quilting and variegated pearl cotton for "big-stitch" circles.

"This quilt will never win a master quiltmaker award," Mary says. "The title says it all for me and if people don't get it, it's still a great bed cover."

Relative Comfort

Finished Size
Quilt: 72½" x 82½"
Blocks: 42 (7½" x 7½")

Materials*
21 (9" x 14") light scrap fabrics
19 (9" x 22") fat eighths dark
   scrap fabrics
¾ yard gold fabric
1½ yards light yellow fabric
2¾ yards black fabric
5¼ yards backing fabric
*Note: As in all scrap quilts,
these yardages are recommendations. Yardage is sufficient to get
1 star and 1 background from
each fabric. Use your own scraps
and fabric placement as desired.

Cutting
Make templates of patterns A–F
on page 17. Cut all strips cross-
grain. Cut pieces in order listed
to make best use of yardage.
When possible, pieces are listed
in order needed, so you don't
have to cut everything all at once.
From light scrap fabrics
- 42 sets of 4 Bs (2 sets from
  each fabric).
From each dark scrap fabric
- 7 (3") sashing squares (127
  total).
- 14 of Pattern C (254 total).
From gold fabric
- 4 (3"-wide) strips. From these,
  cut 56 (3") sashing squares.
- 4 (2¼"-wide) strips. From
  these, cut 72 of Pattern A
  (2¼" squares).
From light yellow fabric
- 16 (3"-wide) strips. From
  these, cut 224 (3") sashing
  squares.

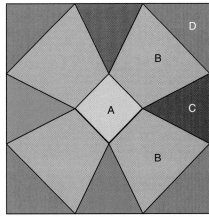

Maltese Cross Block—Make 42.

From black fabric
- 7 (3⅜"-wide) strips. From
  these, cut 84 (3⅜") squares.
  Cut each square in half diagonally to get 168 D triangles.
- 56 of Pattern E.
- 30 of Pattern F and 30 of
  Pattern F reversed.
- 2 (2⅛") squares. Cut each
  square in half diagonally to get
  4 G triangles for corner
  blocks.
- 1 (30") square for binding.

Quilt Assembly
1. For each block, choose 1 A
square, 1 set of 4 matching B
pieces, and 4 D triangles. Don't
worry about C pieces just yet.
2. Sew a B piece onto each edge
of A square, being careful to
start and stop each seam ¼"

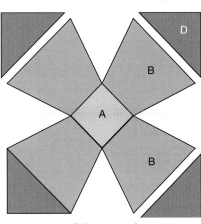

Diagram A

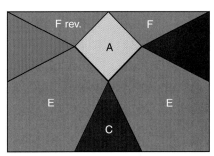

Half-Block—Make 26.

Corner Block—Make 4.

from each corner of A square
(Diagram A). Press seam allowances toward Bs.
3. Sew a D triangle to end of
each B piece as shown. Press
seam allowances toward Ds.
4. Make 42 blocks without Cs.
5. Referring to photograph, lay
out 7 horizontal rows on floor
with 6 blocks in each row.
6. Sew 2 light yellow squares to
opposite sides of each gold
square. Press seam allowances
toward gold. Add 56 (3-square)
units to layout in horizontal rows
between block rows, leaving

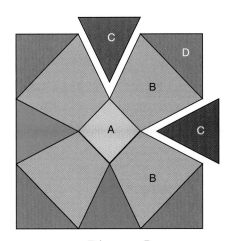

Diagram B

spaces for colored squares.

7. Place colored squares and C pieces in layout. In quilt shown, "circles" are color-coordinated by placing a colored square between 2 Cs of similar color.

8. When satisfied with placement, set Cs into each block *(Diagram B)*. Press seam allowances toward Bs. Complete 42 blocks, returning each finished block to layout.

9. For sashing units between blocks, sew a light yellow square to 2 opposite sides of colored square. Press seam allowances toward colored squares.

10. Assemble each block row, alternating sashing units and blocks as shown in photo.

11. Complete sashing rows, joining colored squares between yellow 3-square units. Press seam allowances toward colored squares.

12. Return all units to layout.

13. For each half-block, join Es to 2 adjacent sides of A square. Sew F and F reversed to remaining sides *(Half-Block Diagram)*. Set in selected Cs. Add half-blocks to ends of block rows and add half-block border rows at top and bottom of layout.

14. For each corner block, sew an E to 1 edge of A and a G triangle to opposite edge *(Corner Block Diagram)*. Sew F and F reversed pieces to remaining sides of A. Set in selected Cs. Add corner blocks to ends of top and bottom border rows.

15. When satisfied with layout, join all horizontal block rows and sashing rows, including half-block border rows. Return assembled rows to layout to verify correct position.

16. Join all rows to complete quilt top.

16

Quilting and Finishing

1. Assemble backing. Layer backing, batting, and quilt top.

2. Quilt as desired. Quilt shown is hand-quilted with variegated thread to emphasize circles. Sashing squares are outline-quilted with black thread.

3. Make 9 yards of bias or straight-grain binding from reserved fabric. Bind quilt edges.

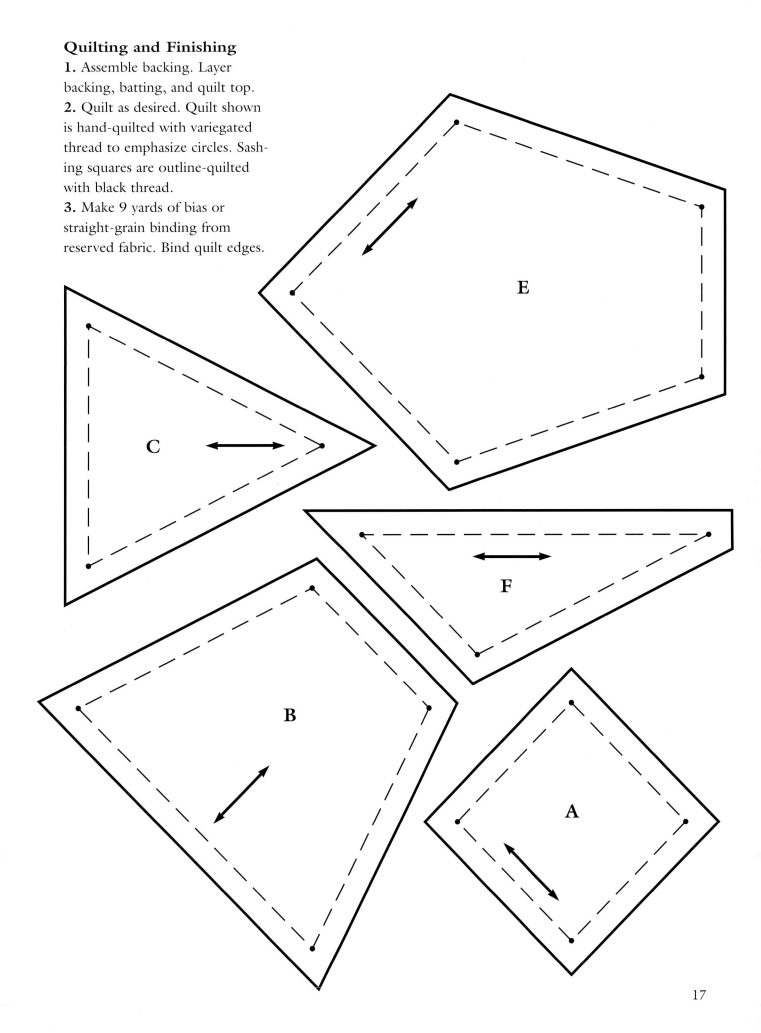

Jean Biddick
Berkeley Heights, New Jersey

*S*ome of Jean Biddick's students affectionately call her "The Queen of Picky Piecing." But Jean doesn't think of her style as being picky. Rather, she says, "There's just something very satisfying about precise piecing."

A quiltmaker for most of her life, Jean started teaching quilting in 1984. "I give students a sound technical basis so they have the skills to support their dreams," she says.

Jean is presently a member of the Garden State Quilter's Guild.

San Diego Sunset
1998

Jean started this quilt with block-of-the-month packets from a quilt shop. She didn't like the blocks, but she loved the batik fabric. So she looked for a nicer block that used the same amount of fabric.

Jean chose the Odd Fellows Chain block because it is also known as San Diego, and Jean lived in that California city when her children were born.

The monthly packets didn't come quickly enough to suit her, so Jean started buying batiks and trading with friends. Each block has just two fabrics, though the variegated colors sometimes makes it seem like more.

Jean used her computer to design the pieced sashing. She chose a graduated wash of yellow, pink, and orange that, with the other fabrics, remind her of sunsets and gave the quilt its name.

San Diego Sunset won a third-place ribbon at the 2000 American Quilter's Society show in Paducah, Kentucky.

San Diego Sunset

Finished Size

Quilt: 73" x 89"

Blocks: 20 (12" x 12")

30 (4" x 4")

Materials*

20 (9" x 22") fat eighths light batik fabrics

20 (9" x 22") fat eighths dark batik fabrics

10 (4" x 7") light scraps for small star blocks

10 (2½" x 10") dark scraps for small star blocks

3 (½-yard) pieces orange and/or pink fabrics for sashing

1½ yards green fabric for sashing

2½ yards gold fabric for lengthwise border strips, or ¾ yard for cross-grain strips

1 yard binding fabric

5½ yards backing fabric

*Note: As in all scrap quilts, these yardages are recommendations. Each fat eighth is enough for 1 large block and 1 small block. Use your own scraps and fabric placement as desired.

Cutting

Instructions are for rotary cutting and traditional piecing. If you prefer traditional cutting, make templates for patterns A–J on page 23.

Cut pieces in order listed to make best use of yardage. When possible, pieces are listed in order needed, so you don't have to cut everything all at once.

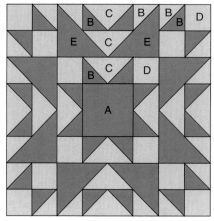

San Diego Block—Make 20.

From each light fat eighth

- 1 (4¼" x 22") strip. From this, cut 3 (4¼") squares. Cut each square in quarters diagonally to get 12 C triangles. From remainder of strip, cut 1 (3¼") square. Cut this square in quarters diagonally to get 4 H triangles.
- 1 (2⅜" x 22") strip. From this, cut 8 (2⅜") squares. Cut each square in half diagonally to get 16 B triangles.
- 12 (2") D squares.
- 4 (1½") J squares.

From each dark fat eighth

- 1 (3⅞" x 22") strip. From this, cut 4 (3⅞") squares. Cut each square in half diagonally to get 8 E triangles. From remainder of strip, cut 1 (3½") A square.
- 1 (2½") F square.
- 12 (2⅜") squares. Cut each square in half diagonally to get 24 B triangles.
- 4 (1⅞") squares. Cut each square in half diagonally to get 8 G triangles.

From each light scrap

- 1 (3¼") square. Cut this square in quarters diagonally to get 4 H triangles.
- 4 (1½") J squares.

Star Block—Make 30.

From each dark scrap

- 1 (2½") F square.
- 4 (1⅞") squares. Cut each square in half diagonally to get 8 G triangles.

From orange/pink sashing fabrics

- 17 (2½" x 42") strips.

From green sashing fabric

- 34 (1½" x 42") strips.

From gold border fabric

- 4 (2¾" x 86") lengthwise strips or 8 (2¾" x 42") cross-grain strips.

Block Assembly

1. For each San Diego block, choose 1 A, 24 B, and 8 E of same dark fabric, as well as 16 B, 12 C, and 12 D of a coordinating light fabric.

2. For center star, sew B triangles to short legs of 4 C triangles (*Diagram A*). Press seam allowances toward Bs. Sew 2 B/C units to opposite sides of A square. Press seam allowances toward A. Sew D squares to both ends of remaining B/C units. Press seam allowances toward Ds; then sew units to opposite sides of A as shown.

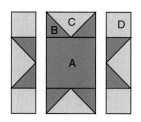

Diagram A

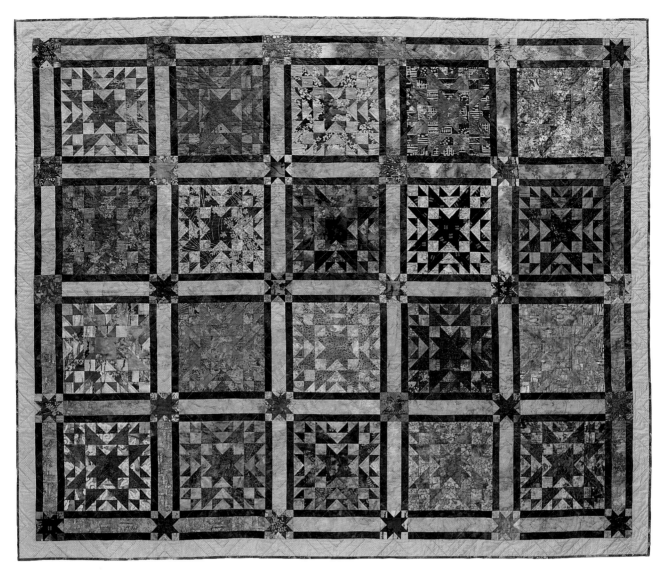

3. For each corner unit, join light and dark B triangles to make 2 triangle-squares *(Diagram B)*. Press seam allowances toward dark fabric. Then sew a D square to dark triangle; press seam allowances toward Ds. Join rows to complete corner unit. Make 4 corner units.

4. For 1 side unit, sew dark Bs to opposite sides of a C triangle *(Diagram C)*. Press seam allowances toward Bs. Sew light Bs to both ends of row; then join a C triangle to bottom of combined unit. Press seam allowances toward light Bs and C. Add E triangles to both sides to complete unit. Make 4 side units.

5. Join units in rows *(Block Assembly Diagram)*. Join rows to complete block.

6. Make 20 blocks.

7. Use 1 set of light H and J pieces and 1 set of dark F and G pieces to make each small star block *(Diagram A)*. Make 30 small star blocks.

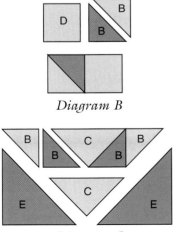

Diagram B

Diagram C

Block Assembly Diagram

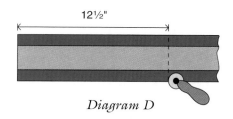

12½"

Diagram D

Quilt Assembly

1. Sew a green sashing strip to both sides of each pink/orange sashing strip *(Diagram D)*. Make 17 strip sets. Press all seam allowances toward green.

2. Cut 3 (12½"-wide) segments from each strip set to get a total of 49 segments.

3. Lay out blocks in 5 horizontal rows with 4 blocks in each row *(Row Assembly Diagram)*. Arrange blocks to achieve a pleasing balance of color and pattern. Place sashing units between blocks and at both ends of each row.

4. Lay out remaining sashing units in 6 rows at top, bottom, and between block rows, alternating sashing units with small star blocks *(Row Assembly Diagram)*.

5. When satisfied with placement of blocks, join blocks and sashing in each row. Press seam

allowances toward sashing units in all rows.

6. Join rows, alternating sashing rows and block rows.

Borders

1. Measure length of quilt top through middle of pieced section. Trim 2 border strips to match quilt length. Sew borders to quilt sides, easing to fit as needed. Press seam allowances toward borders.

2. Measure width of quilt top through middle, including side borders. Trim remaining borders to match width. Sew borders to top and bottom edges of quilt, easing to fit as needed. Press seam allowances toward borders.

Quilting and Finishing

1. Assemble backing. Layer backing, batting, and quilt top.

2. Quilt as desired. Quilt shown is outline-quilted with variegated embroidery floss; diagonal lines of quilting extend into sashing and borders.

3. Make 9¼ yards of bias or straight-grain binding from reserved fabric. Bind quilt edges.

Sashing Row—Make 6.

Block Row—Make 5.

Row Assembly Diagram

❖QUILT SMART❖
Quilting Supplies & Resources

If you're looking for fabric, supplies, or books not available at your local shops, contact these companies for free catalogs or product information.

Big Horn Quilts
P.O. Box 566
Greybull, WY 82426
1-877-586-9150
www.BigHornQuilts.com

Fabric Loft of New England
(specializing in one-piece backing fabrics)
P.O. Box 43
East Hampton, CT 06424
1-860-365-0102
www.FabricLoft.com

Family Treasures
(¹⁄₁₆"-diameter hole punch, Product #3271-01)
24922 Anza Drive, Unit A
Valencia, CA 91355
1-800-413-2645

Hancock's of Paducah
3841 Hinkleville Road
Paducah, KY 42001
1-800-845-8723
www.Hancocks-Paducah.com

Keepsake Quilting™
P.O. Box 1618
Centre Harbor, NH 03226
1-800-865-9458
www.keepsakequilting.com

Oxmoor House
1-800-633-4910
www.oxmoorhouse.com

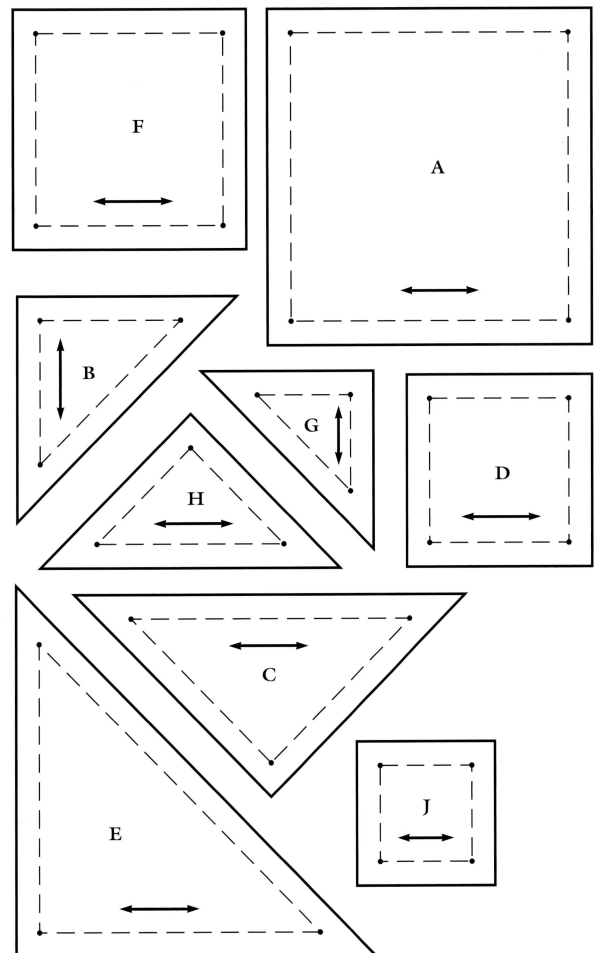

F

A

B

G

D

H

C

E

J

Lois Pio
Hermosa Beach, California

*T*hough she's making an heirloom quilt for each of her grandchildren (six quilts done, four to go), Lois Pio has a real passion for art quilts.

"Making quilts for comfort is important," Lois says, "but art quilts make me stretch." Designing with color and cloth satisfies Lois's need for expression. She particularly likes scrap quilts and placing traditional blocks in contemporary and original settings.

"I'm happiest when I'm hand piecing or hand quilting."

Lois took her first quilting class at the UCLA extension in 1984 and never looked back. She continues to take classes to keep up with new techniques and trends. "I'm happiest when I'm hand piecing or hand quilting," Lois says. "But I will use the machine for certain tasks."

Lois is a member of Quilts on the Wall, Fiber Artists, and the South Bay Quilters Guild.

Careening & Circling
2000

Lois Pio decided to make these Drunkard's Path blocks one day, "just to use up scraps," she says.

Lois wanted to create an original set for the simple traditional blocks, so she kept moving them around until she came up with a block layout that she liked.

"I like the challenge of using traditional blocks in interesting ways," she says.

When the quilt top was finished, Lois cut fabric circles of varying size and, with the encouragement of a friend, literally tossed them onto the top. "The randomness of appliquéing them down where they landed was a freeing experience," she says.

Careening & Circling was shown at the South Bay Quilters Guild show in February 2001, and at the Cypress Community Gallery in July and July of 2000.

Careening & Circling

Finished Size
Quilt: 50½" x 62½"
Blocks: 204 (3" x 3")

Materials*
2½" squares print scrap fabrics
as follows:
36 violet/purple
30 blue
26 tan/brown
24 yellow
24 red/pink
24 green
24 teal/turquoise
16 peach/orange/rust
28 scrap fabrics for appliquéd
circles, 2"–3½" square
38 (1"-wide) scrap strips, from
10" to 14" long, for inner
border and pieced binding
2¾ yards muslin
3¼ yards backing fabric
* *Note:* Because scraps in this
quilt are so small and varied, it
is impractical to specify yardage.
Materials listed above are to
make quilt as shown. Use your
own scraps and color placement
as desired.

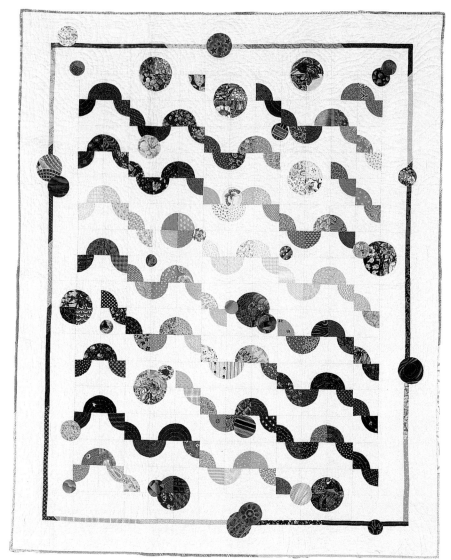

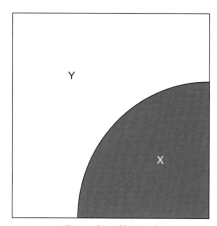

*Drunkard's Path
Block—Make 204.*

Cutting
Make templates of patterns X, Y,
and circles on page 29. As much
as possible, cutting is listed in
order needed, so you don't have
to cut everything all at once.
From 2½" scrap squares
• 204 of Template X.
From muslin
• 6 (3½"-wide) cross-grain
strips. From these, cut 72 of
Template Y.
• 2 (4"-wide) cross-grain strips
for top and bottom borders.
• 2 (4"x 64") lengthwise strips
for borders.
• 8 (3½" x 64") lengthwise
strips. From these, cut 132 of
Template Y.

• 2 (3½" x 64") lengthwise
strips. From these and remaining strip from previous step,
cut 2 (3½" x 24½") A strips,
2 (3½" x 18½") B strips,
3 (3½" x 12½") D strips,
2 (3½" x 9½") C strips, and 1
(3½" x 6½") E strip.

Block Assembly
See Quilt Smart, opposite, for
tips on sewing a curved seam.
Sew each X to a muslin Y. Make
204 Drunkard's Path blocks.

continued

❖QUILT SMART❖

Piecing a Curved Seam

Curved piecing isn't as difficult as many people seem to fear. It just requires a little extra care to ensure a smooth, accurate seam. Try making a few practice units, using the methods described here, to see which technique you like best.

Hand or Machine Piecing

1. On each Y piece, make small clips between dots shown on pattern. Be careful not to cut into seam line. Clips allow seam allowance to spread so curved edges will match for piecing.

2. Match an X and a Y, right sides facing. Pin curved edges together, match-ing dots *(Dia-gram A)*. Let Y gather as neces-sary, but make it as smooth as possible at curved edge.

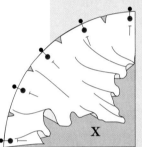

Diagram A

3. With Y on top, stitch curved seam. Start at one end and carefully sew around curve, smoothing creas-es away from seam as you go. Remove each pin before you sew over it.

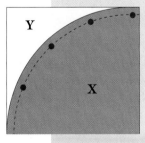

Diagram B

4. Press seam allowances toward Y *(Dia-gram B)*. If necessary, a hot iron can work out tiny puck-ers in the seam.

Appliqué

1. Make a pressing template for piece X. Use Templar (a heat-resistant, translucent sheet avail-able at quilt shops) or a light-weight aluminum such as the bottom of a disposable pie pan. Cut template with seam allow-ances on straight edges but not on curves *(Diagram C)*.

2. Place fabric X piece facedown on ironing board. Spray curved edge with water or spray starch. Place template on fabric, align-ing straight edges *(Diagram D)*. Use tip of iron to press curved seam allowance over template edge. (If using aluminum, keep fingers away from template—metal will be hot at pressed edge.) Remove template when seam allowance is dry.

3. Pin X to Y, aligning straight edges *(Diagram E)*. Using thread that matches X, appliqué curved edge with a hand blind-stitch *(Diagram F)* or machine topstitch *(Diagram G)*.

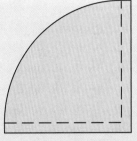

Diagram C

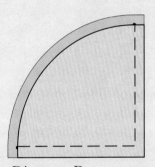

Diagram D

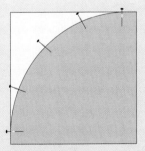

Diagram E

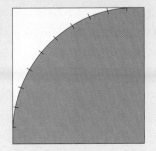

Diagram F

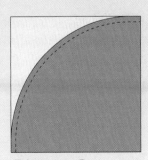

Diagram G

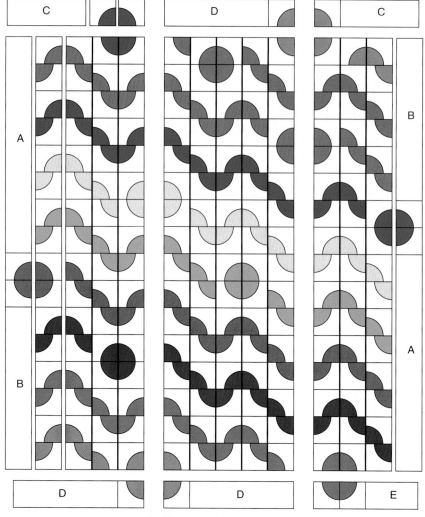

Quilt Assembly Diagram

Quilt Assembly

1. Lay out blocks in 12 vertical rows, with 16 blocks in each row (*Quilt Assembly Diagram*). Place A and B strips at sides, inserting block pairs as shown. Place C and D strips at top, D and E strips at bottom, inserting blocks. If you prefer an arrangement different than that shown, feel free to do your own thing.

2. When satisfied with placement of blocks, join blocks and strips in each side row; then join remaining vertical rows.

3. Join vertical rows in 3 sections as shown.

4. Join strips and blocks in top row and bottom rows by section. Join assembled units to top and bottom edges of each section.

5. Join sections.

Borders

1. For inner border, join 18 (1"-wide) scrap strips end-to-end with diagonal seams.

2. Measure length of quilt top through middle of pieced section. Cut 2 inner border strips to match length. Sew borders to quilt sides, easing to fit.

3. Measure width of quilt top through middle, including side borders. Trim 2 inner border strips to match width. Sew borders to top and bottom edges of quilt, easing to fit as needed.

4. Repeat steps 2 and 3 to add muslin borders.

Quilting and Finishing

1. From remaining 28 scrap squares, cut circles in assorted sizes (see patterns on facing page). Place circles on quilt as desired, placing some across border seams as shown. Hand-appliqué circles in place.

2. Layer backing, batting, and quilt top.

3. Quilt as desired. Quilt shown is outline-quilted with wavy lines quilted through each X, connecting each color family. Echo-quilting fills in Ys and border.

4. Join remaining 1"-wide strips end-to-end with diagonal seams. On 1 long edge of strip, press under ¼". Matching right sides and raw edges, sew unpressed edge to right side of quilt. Turn binding over quilt edge. Hand-stitch pressed fold to backing.

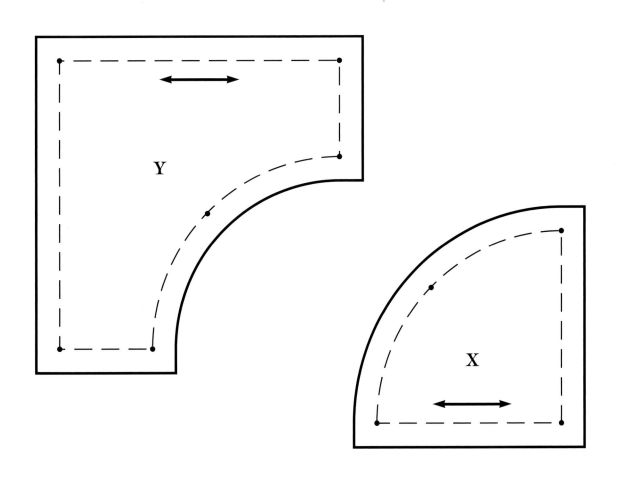

Y

X

Circle Patterns for Appliqué

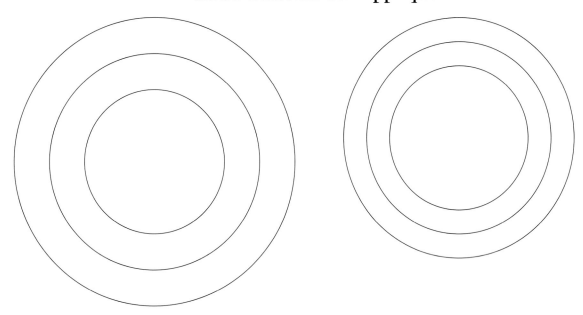

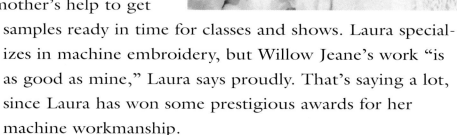

Laura Heine
Billings, Montana
Willow Jeane Lyman
Alexandria, Virginia

*L*aura Heine and her mother, Willow Jeane Lyman, live far apart, but they say that making quilts together helps bridge the distance between them.

Because of her busy schedule, Laura sometimes needs her mother's help to get

> *"I'll ask (my mom) to finish a quilt I've started so I can move on to the next project."*

samples ready in time for classes and shows. Laura specializes in machine embroidery, but Willow Jeane's work "is as good as mine," Laura says proudly. That's saying a lot, since Laura has won some prestigious awards for her machine workmanship.

Laura's success as quiltmaker, designer, and teacher didn't happen overnight. In 1985, she was a registered nurse and expecting her first child when she took a quilting class. "I wanted to make one quilt in my life," she says. "I figured that once the baby came, my chance would be lost."

But Laura won an award with her very first quilt. "I was so excited, and then I realized I was the only entrant in that division!" she recalls. "Still, I was hooked." In 1994, after many more quilts and awards, Laura gave up nursing and became the owner of Fiberworks, a quilt shop in Billings.

Visit Laura's website at fiberworks-heine.com to see her other patterns and the luscious floral fabrics she designs for King's Road.

Folk Art Flowers & Flies
2000

So many quilts, so little time—that was Laura Heine's problem. Already working on the next design, Laura sent *Folk Art Flowers & Flies* to her mother to finish the machine embroidery. "I can't even tell what I did and what she did," Laura says.

This quilt is Laura's original design, one in a series of quilts featuring flowers. The appliqué, embroidery, and quilting are done by machine.

Folk Art Flowers & Flies was exhibited at International Quilt Festival 2000 in Houston, Texas.

Folk Art Flowers & Flies

Finished Size
Quilt: 82" x 82"
Blocks: 9 (19" x 19")

Materials*
3 yards navy fabric for blocks
2½ yards mottled blue fabric for flying geese units and border
¼ yard dark purple for sashing squares
Assorted scraps (yellow, orange, red, purple, blue, teal, green) for flying geese units
⅞ yard binding fabric
5 yards backing fabric
Freezer paper (optional for hand or machine appliqué)
Embroidery floss or machine embroidery thread in colors to match appliqué fabrics (optional)

Flower Blocks
5 (9" x 22") fat eighths assorted yellow-green prints for leaves
½ yard emerald green for flower
⅜ yard red print for flower
⅓ yard purple for flower
⅛ yard gold for flower

Butterfly Blocks
4 (¼-yard) pieces dark prints for large wing sections
4 (9" x 22") fat eighths assorted prints for small wing sections
4 (4" x 11") scraps for bodies
¼ yard red for border flange
8 (⅜"-diameter) buttons
* *Note:* As in all scrap quilts, these yardages are recommendations. Use your own scraps and fabric placement as desired.

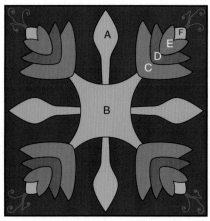

Flower Block—Make 5.

Butterfly Block—Make 4.

Cutting
Make templates of patterns A–L on pages 34 to 38. Cut pieces in order listed to make best use of yardage. When possible, pieces are listed in order needed, so you don't have to cut everything all at once.

From navy fabric
• 9 (20") squares for blocks.

From freezer paper
Trace templates onto dull side of freezer paper and cut:
• 20 of Template A.
• 5 of Template B.
• 20 *each* of templates C, D, E, and F.
• 4 *each* of templates G, G reversed, H, H reversed, J, J reversed, K, K reversed, and L.
Apply cut pieces to appliqué fabrics and cut appliqué pieces, adding seam allowance around outside edges of each paper piece. Set aside remaining freezer paper for flying geese units.

From each yellow-green print
• 1 of Template B.
• 4 of Template A.

From emerald green fabric
• 20 of Pattern C.

From red print fabric
• 20 of Pattern D.

From purple fabric
• 20 of Pattern E.

From gold fabric
• 20 of Pattern F.

From each dark print
• 1 of Template G and 1 of Template G reversed.
• 1 of Template J and 1 of Template J reversed.

From each assorted print fabric
• 1 of Template H and 1 of Template H reversed.
• 1 of Template K and 1 of Template K reversed.

From each scrap fabric
• 1 of Template L.

From red fabric
• 16 (1" x 20") strips for flange.

From mottled blue fabric
• 4 (6" x 85") lengthwise strips for outer borders. Set aside remaining mottled fabric and assorted scraps for flying geese border.

From dark purple fabric
• 16 (4") sashing squares.

Block Assembly

Quilt shown was appliquéd by machine, using decorative stitches and embroidery thread to coordinate with each fabric. You can appliqué by hand and add embroidery later, or you can eliminate embroidery.

1. For each flower block, select 1 navy square, 4 A pieces, and 1 B piece of same green fabric or different fabric, as desired. Fold square in half vertically, horizontally, and diagonally, making creases for appliqué placement guides *(Diagram A)*. Turn A and B edges over freezer paper and press, clipping seam allowance to get smooth curves.

2. Center B on square, aligning its arms with diagonal creases. Align A pieces with vertical and horizontal lines, slipping ends under B. Pin. Appliqué As and B

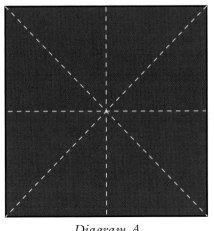

Diagram A

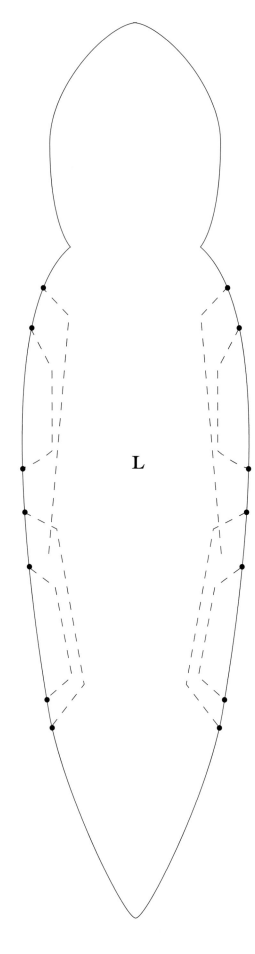

L

in place by hand or by machine.

3. Prepare edges of 4 sets of flower pieces (C, D, E, and F). Appliqué pieces in alphabetical order on each arm of B.

4. For each butterfly block, select 1 navy square, and 1 each of pieces G, G reversed, H, H reversed, J, J reversed, K, K reversed, and L. Fold square in half vertically and horizontally, making creases for appliqué placement guides. Turn appliqué edges over freezer paper and press, clipping seam allowance to get smooth curves.

5. Center L piece on block; then position wing pieces, slipping ends under L. Pin. Appliqué pieces in alphabetical order. Add antenna embroidery.

6. Make 5 flower blocks and 4 butterfly blocks. When appliqué is complete, trim navy fabric from behind appliqué pieces, leaving ¼" seam allowances. Carefully remove freezer paper.

7. Press each block. Measuring from center, square up and trim each block to 19½" square.

8. Press each flange strip in half lengthwise, wrong sides facing. Matching raw edges, baste a strip onto each edge of each butterfly block, overlapping corners. Trim strips even with sides of block.

Quilt Assembly

In the quilt shown, the flying geese units are not uniform. We've provided 3 variations on pages 36 and 37. You can create more, if you like, varying height and angle of each center triangle. Each unit must be 3½" wide (plus seam allowances), and the 5 or 6 units joined for each sashing strip must add up to 19" (plus seam allowances at each end of strip).

1. Draw or trace 5 or 6 flying geese units (depending on height) onto freezer paper. Cut apart triangles in each unit. Press side triangles onto mottled blue fabric and center triangles onto scrap fabrics. (*Note:* In quilt shown, center triangles in each sashing strip are more or less grouped by color.) Cut out triangles, adding ¼" seam allowance around each paper piece.

2. Join triangles in each unit. Press seam allowances toward blue triangles. Then join triangles end-to-end to make a sashing strip 19" long (plus seam allowances at each end of strip). Remove freezer paper from back of each unit.

3. Make 24 sashing strips.

4. Referring to photograph, lay out blocks and sashing strips in horizontal rows, with 3 blocks and 4 sashing strips in each row. Lay out sashing rows between block rows, placing dark purple sashing squares between sashing strips as shown. Arrange blocks and sashing strips to achieve a nice balance of color.

5. When satisfied with placement of blocks and sashing, join units in each row. (Flange strips on Butterfly Blocks will be sewn into joining seams.) Press.

6. Join rows.

7. Add embroidery at tip of each flower, extending design into sashing. Add embroidery embellishments to flying geese units, if desired. (Willow Jeane had fun stitching zigzags and doodles on sashing units.)

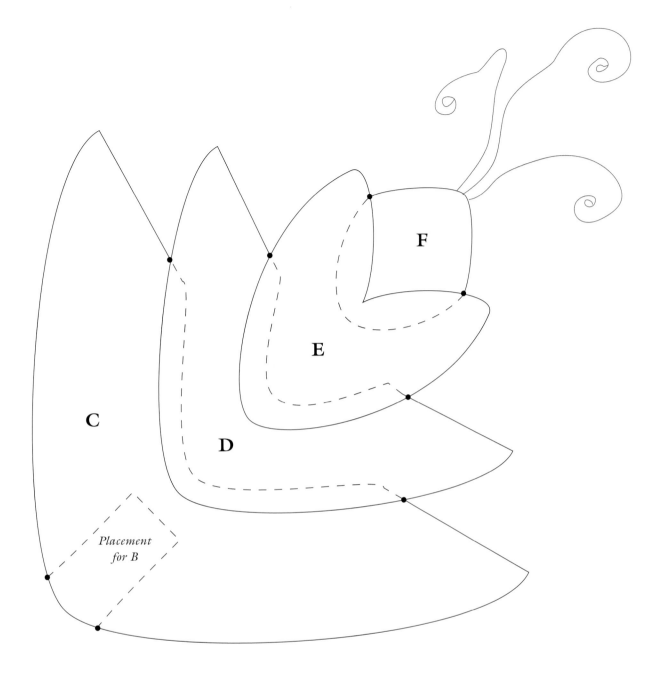

C

F

E

D

*Placement
for B*

Borders

1. Measure length of quilt top through middle of pieced section. Trim 2 border strips to match quilt length. Sew borders to quilt sides, easing to fit as needed. Press seam allowances toward borders.

2. Measure width of quilt top through middle, including side borders. Trim 2 border strips to match width. Sew borders to top and bottom edges of quilt, easing to fit as needed. Press seam allowances toward borders.

Quilting and Finishing

1. Assemble backing. Layer backing, batting, and quilt top.

2. Quilt as desired. Quilt shown is machine-quilted with stippling in background of each block, stitched with variegated thread. Borders are quilted from the back, following the floral design of the backing fabric.

3. Sew button eyes onto each butterfly.

4. Make 9½ yards of bias or straight-grain binding from reserved fabric. (Binding on quilt shown is a multi-colored print. For a similar look, you can cut 2½"-wide strips of scrap fabrics and piece them end-to-end to make 9½ yards of straight-grain binding.) Bind quilt edges.

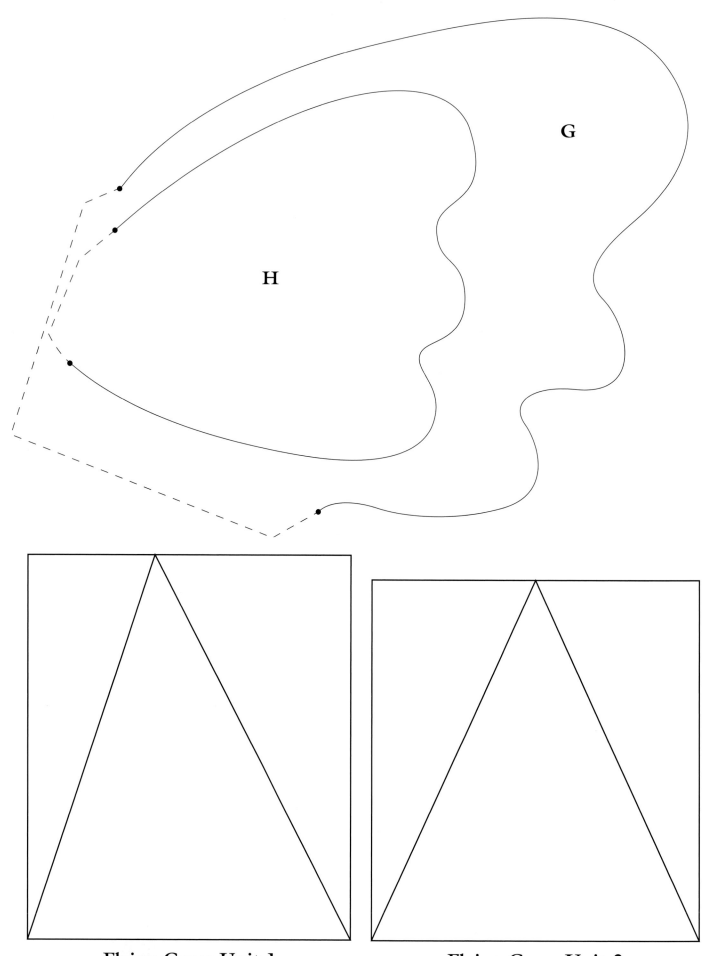

G

H

Flying Geese Unit 1

Flying Geese Unit 2

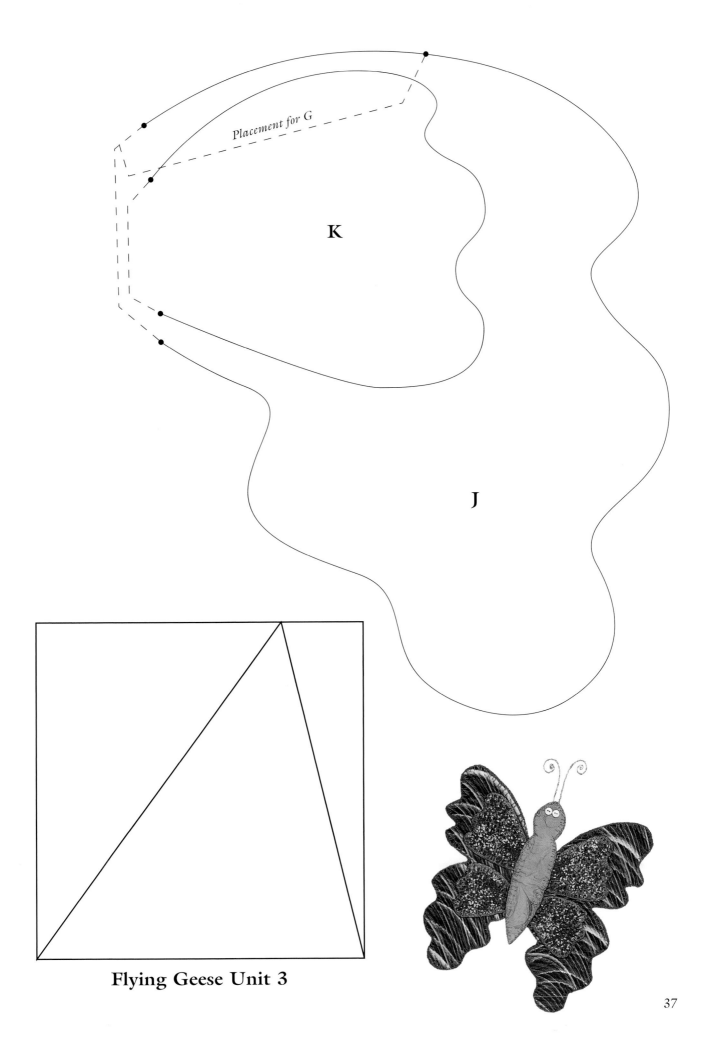

Placement for G

K

J

Flying Geese Unit 3

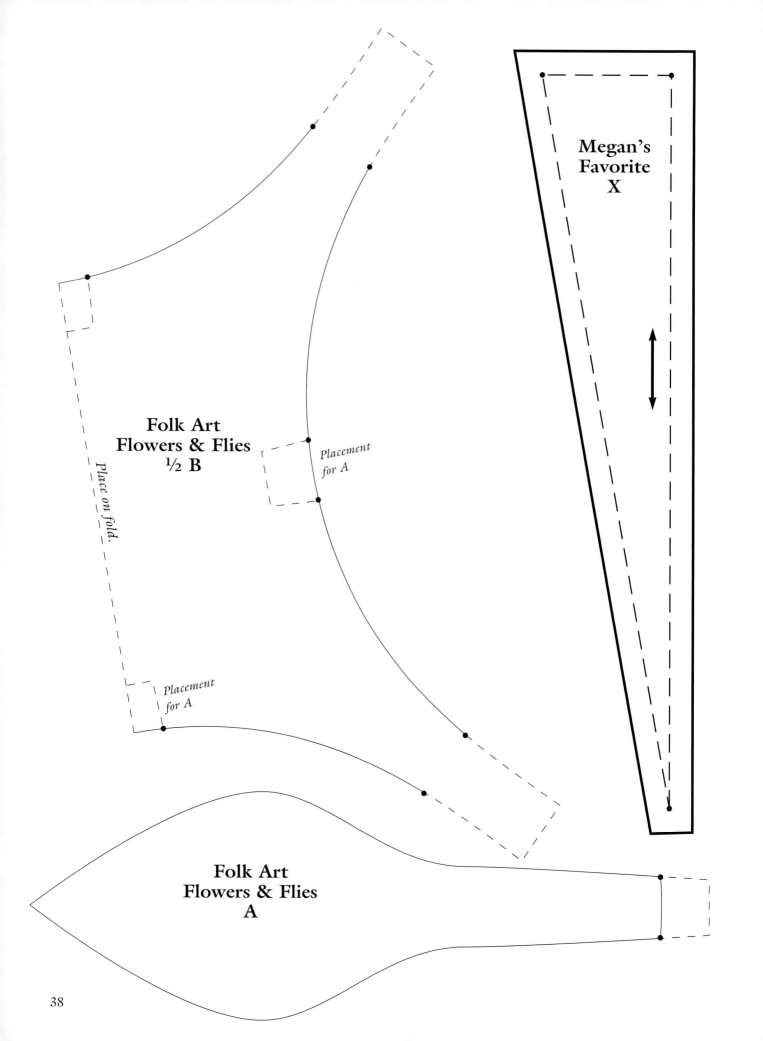

**Megan's
Favorite
X**

**Folk Art
Flowers & Flies
½ B**

Place on fold.

*Placement
for A*

*Placement
for A*

**Folk Art
Flowers & Flies
A**

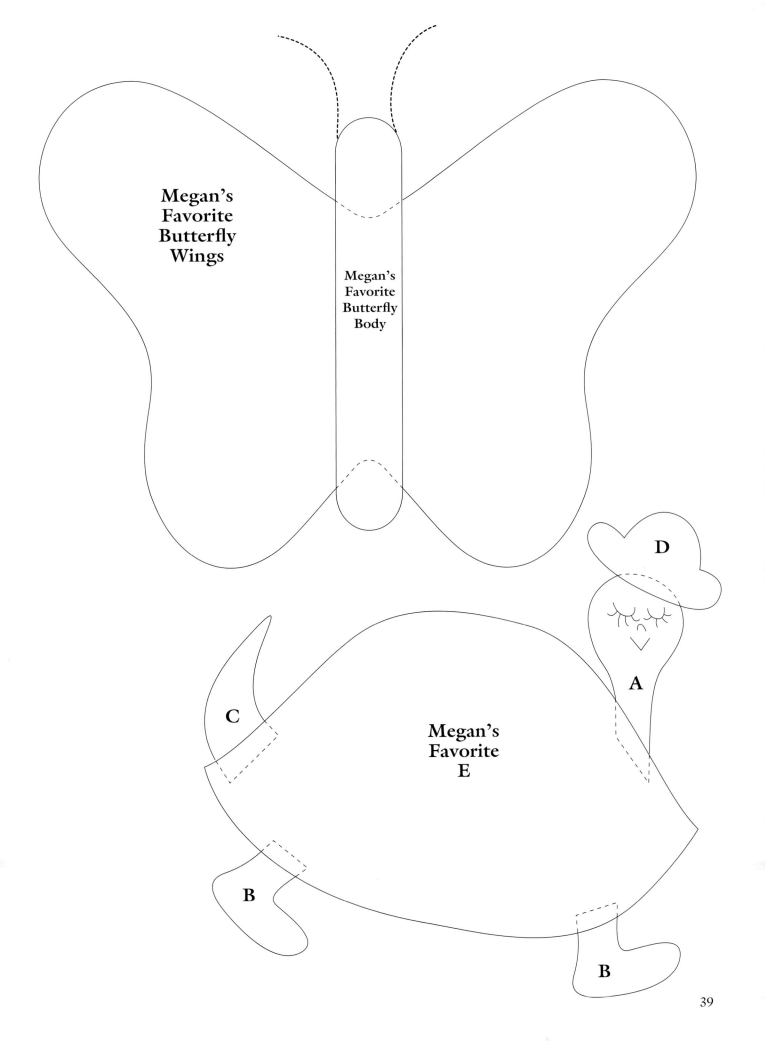

Megan's
Favorite
Butterfly
Wings

Megan's
Favorite
Butterfly
Body

D

A

C

Megan's
Favorite
E

B

B

Karen DuMont
Richmond, Virginia

I like to sew, dough, and hoe," says Karen DuMont, describing her three favorite pastimes.

Karen began quilting soon after her family moved to Richmond in 1992. She also designs all-occasion dough ornaments and jewelry, which she sells at craft fairs and on-line at www.adoughables.com. And she's an avid gardener.

Karen shares her love of these things with her daughter, Megan, a teacher. "It gives me comfort to know that I'll pass on my knowledge and talents," Karen says.

"It gives me comfort to know that I'll pass on my knowledge."

Karen and Megan are getting other family members involved in quilting. They've started a family quilt camp, inviting relatives of all ages to share a fun get-away. "We've been teaching the basics of cutting and assembling," Karen says. "Most importantly, we encourage imagination, design, and working together." Sharing ideas and learning new skills is one of the reasons Karen loves making quilts. "Quilting lets me use my imagination, working with color and texture," she says.

Karen is a member of the the Bon Air Sewing Sisters and the James River Heritage Quilters.

Megan's Favorite
2000

When Karen DuMont's daughter, Megan, a fourth-grade teacher, asked Karen to make a fun, colorful quilt for her classroom, Karen started playing with scraps and thinking about designs.

Megan's collection of turtles inspired Karen to create the turtle design. "I didn't think I could draw, but this turtle just happened," Karen says. She had fun giving each turtle a different personality.

While she was planning the quilt, Karen helped plant a flower garden at Megan's new home, so the posies and butterflies seemed natural additions to Megan's quilt.

This quilt never made it to school, but a smaller version of it hangs there for Megan's students to enjoy.

Megan's Favorite was shown at the Richmond Quilters' Guild 2000 show.

Megan's Favorite

Finished Size
Quilt: 59" x 59"
Blocks: 25 (9" x 9")

Materials*
16 (9" x 22") fat eighths bright print scrap fabrics
1 (9" x 22") fat eighth black fabric for butterflies
1⅜ yards white fabric
½ yard blue print border fabric
1¾ yards pink print border fabric (includes binding)
3¾ yards backing fabric
Fine-tipped permanent markers for turtle faces
Scraps of embroidery floss for butterfly antennae
* *Note:* These yardages and the cutting instructions below are recommendations for efficient purchase of yardage. Use your own scraps and fabric placement as desired before deciding what additional fabric to purchase.

Cutting
Make templates of turtle, butterfly, and X patterns on pages 38 and 39 and flower pattern, opposite. Cut pieces in order listed to make best use of yardage.

From scrap fabrics
• 7 of Butterfly Wings template.
• 7 of Flower template.
• 7 of Turtle E template.
• 8 of Flower Center template.
• 1 each of Turtle A and C templates and 2 of Turtle B to make 1 set. Cut 8 sets.
• 8 of Turtle D template (optional; not all of Karen's turtles are wearing hats).
• 100 of Template X.

From black fabric
• 8 of Butterfly Body template.
From white fabric
• 25 (8¼") squares.
From blue print border fabric
• 1 of Flower template.
• 8 (2" x 26") cross-grain strips for inner border.
From pink print border fabric
• 2 (6" x 62") and 2 (6" x 50") lengthwise border strips.
• 4 (2½" x 63") lengthwise strips for straight-grain binding.
• 1 of Butterfly Wings template.
• 1 of Turtle E template.

Block Assembly
1. For Butterfly block, center 1 wings piece on a white square at desired angle (see photo); then center body piece on top. Appliqué by hand or by machine. On quilt shown, Karen DuMont used a machine buttonhole stitch to appliqué butterflies. Make 8 Butterfly blocks. Use scraps of embroidery floss to make antennae with a running stitch.
2. For Flower block, center 1 flower piece on a white square; then position flower center on top. Appliqué. (Karen used a machine satin-stitch to appliqué flowers.) Make 8 Flower blocks.
3. Use fine-tipped permanent marker to trace facial features onto each Turtle A piece.
4. For Turtle block, center an E piece on a white square. Position 1 A, 2 Bs, and 1 C, tucking ends under E. Appliqué. (Karen used a machine buttonhole stitch). Add D hat (optional). Make 9 Turtle blocks.
5. Karen's quilt has scattered small butterfly and bug appliqués

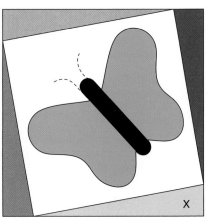
Butterfly Block—Make 8.

Flower Block—Make 8.

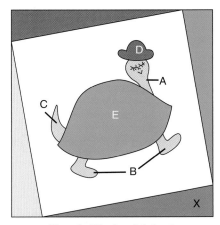
Turtle Block—Make 9.

that she cut out of a novelty print fabric. Add additional appliqués if desired.
6. Select 4 X pieces for each block. Sew X pieces to all sides of block. Press seam allowances toward X pieces.

Quilt Assembly

1. Referring to photo, lay out blocks in 5 horizontal rows with 5 blocks in each row. Arrange blocks to achieve a pleasing balance of color and pattern. When satisifed with placement of blocks, join blocks in each row.
2. Join rows.

Borders

1. Join 2 bright blue strips end-to-end to make a border strip for each edge of quilt.
2. Measure length of quilt top through middle of pieced section. Trim 2 border strips to match quilt length. Sew borders to quilt sides, easing to fit as needed. Press seam allowances toward borders.
3. Measure width of quilt top through middle, including side borders. Trim remaining blue borders to match width. Sew borders to top and bottom edges of quilt. Press seam allowances toward borders.
4. Repeat steps 2 and 3 to add pink outer borders to quilt top.

Quilting and Finishing

1. Assemble backing. Layer backing, batting, and quilt top.
2. Quilt as desired. Quilt shown is machine-quilted with an all-over pattern.
3. Make 7 yards of straight-grain binding from reserved pink strips. Bind quilt edges.

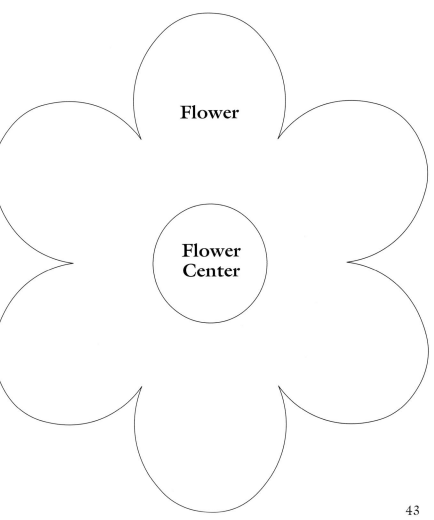

Flower

Flower Center

43

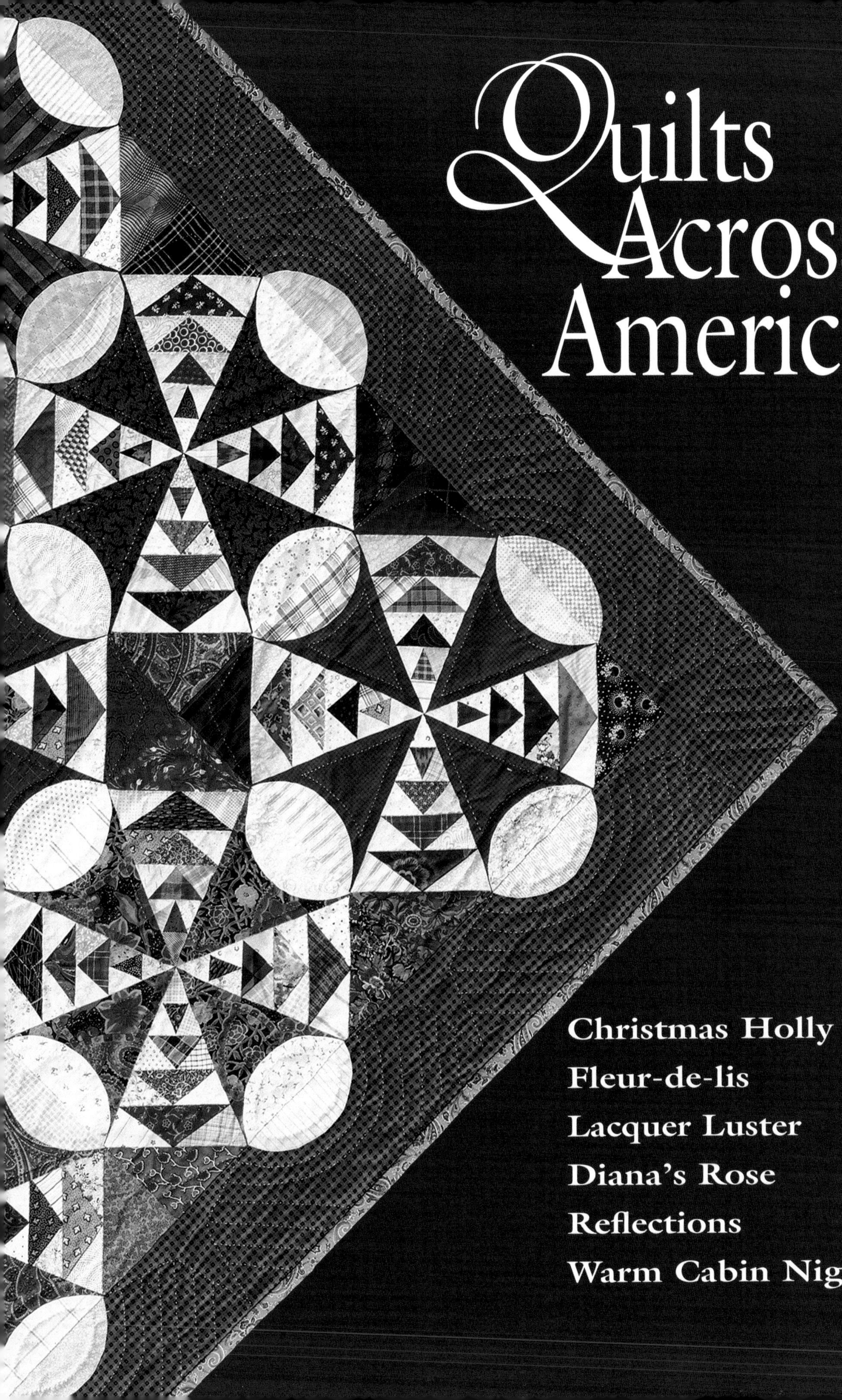

Quilts Across America

Christmas Holly

Fleur-de-lis

Lacquer Luster

Diana's Rose

Reflections

Warm Cabin Nights

Annette Anderson
Ferndale, Washington

*A*nnette Anderson makes no bones about why she loves making quilts. She says, "It's a wonderful excuse to buy fabric."

Of course, being a quiltmaker has other benefits—creative expression and a network of friends. But it's really about fabric. "Today's fabrics are so wonderful, they need to be loved and touched and enjoyed," Annette says.

She's been quilting long enough to remember when the selection of fabrics wasn't as extensive as it is today and the rotary cutter wasn't yet invented. She started in the 1970s with a quilt-as-you-go Log Cabin. Classes and experience have taught Annette the importance of precise pattern drafting and piecing.

Over the years, Annette has dabbled with art quilts and original design, but keeps coming back to the scrappy traditional quilts she loves.

Christmas Holly
1998

As traditional patchwork evolved, quiltmakers created and named designs for familiar things, like baskets, stars, and flowers. This Dusty Miller block is named for a long-stemmed silver-gray plant with complex, spiky leaves.

Annette Anderson drafted a pattern of this challenging block from a picture she saw of a similar quilt. When her quilt was done, she thought the combination of colors and design looked like prickly holly in Chrismas colors.

Though not as familiar as some other blocks, the first known publication of Dusty Miller was in the late 1920s.

Christmas Holly

Finished Size

Quilt: 91" x 91"
Blocks: 36 (13½" x 13½")

Materials*

36 (18" x 22") fat quarters light
    scrap fabrics
36 (18" x 22") fat quarters dark
    scrap fabrics
2⅝ yards border fabric
⅞ yard binding fabric
2⅞ yards 104"-wide backing
144 (8") squares lightweight
    translucent paper (optional;
    see piecing instructions)

*Note: As in all scrap quilts,
these yardages are recommendations. Use your own scraps and
fabric placement as desired. Add
leftover border fabric to scraps, if
desired.

Cutting

Make templates of patterns A–G,
X, and Y on pages 50 and 51.
Use a 1/16"-diameter hole punch
to punch out corner dots on each
template. (See page 22 for a
mail-order source for this punch.)

Cut pieces in order listed to
make best use of yardage. When
possible, pieces are listed in
order needed, so you don't have
to cut everything all at once.

From light fabrics

• 168 of Template Y.
• 432 of Template A.
• 144 of Template B and 144 of
  Template B reversed.
• 144 of Template D and 144 of
  Template D reversed.
• 144 of Template F and 144 of
  Template F reversed.

From each dark fabric

• 4 of Template X.

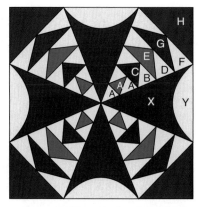

Dusty Miller Block—Make 36.

• 2 (4⅞") squares. Cut each
  square in half diagonally to get
  4 H triangles.
• 4 *each* of Templates A, C, E,
  and G.

From border fabric

• 2 (5½" x 94") and 2 (5½" x
  84") lengthwise strips.

Traditional Block Assembly

1. For each block, choose 4 X
pieces of same fabric, 12 light A
pieces, and 4 *each* of Y, dark As,
B, B reversed, C, D, D reversed,
E, F, F reversed, G, and H.
2. Piece curved X/Y seams. (If
you prefer, turn under Y's
curved seam allowance and
appliqué it onto X.) Press 4
completed X/Y units.
3. For each alternating unit, lay
out A–G triangles in rows (*Block
Assembly Diagram*). Join triangles in each row, matching corner dots on wrong side of each
seam. Press. Join rows to complete A–G unit. Press 4 completed units.
4. Sew an X/Y unit to left side
of each A–G unit. Join 2 pairs to
make a half-block; then join half-
blocks. Press seam allowances
toward X. Add H triangles at
corners to complete block.
5. Make 36 blocks.

Paper Foundation Piecing Block Assembly

1. Follow steps 1 and 2 as
described for Traditional Block
Assembly.
2. Trace complete A–G unit
(page 50) onto an 8"-square of
paper.
3. Pin dark A in place (right side
up) on 1 side of tracing, letting
seam allowances extend over
drawn seam lines. With right
sides facing, stitch light As in
place on sides and top of dark A,
sewing directly on drawn lines
on wrong side of paper (*Block
Assembly Diagram*). Press A
pieces to right side.
4. Match long edge of C to bottom of A unit, right sides facing.
Stitch C through all layers. Press
to right side. Add B and B reversed triangles in same manner.
5. Continue adding rows of triangles, stitching dark triangle of
each row in place first and then
adding light triangles at sides.
Press. Complete 4 A–G units for
each block.
6. See Traditional Block Assembly, Step 4, to complete block.
Make 36 blocks.

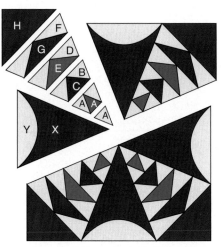

Dusty Miller Block—Make 36.

7. Before continuing, carefully remove papers along perforations made by stitching lines.

Quilt Assembly

1. Lay out blocks in 6 horizontal rows with 6 blocks in each row. Arrange blocks to achieve a pleasing balance of color and pattern.

2. When satisifed with placement of blocks, join blocks in each row. Then join rows.

Borders

1. Turn under curved seam allowance on each remaining Y piece. Press. Matching raw edges and right sides, pin or baste a Y piece on top of each Y piece around outer edge of quilt.

2. Measure length of quilt top through middle of pieced section. Trim 2 (94"-long) border strips to match quilt length.

3. Sew borders to quilt sides, easing to fit as needed and catching basted Y pieces in seam. Press seam allowances toward borders.

4. Appliqué curved edge of each Y piece in place on side borders.

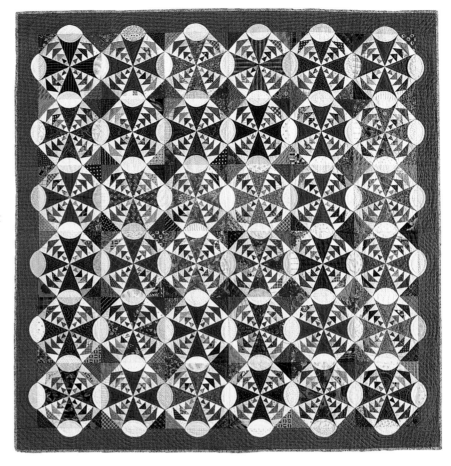

5. Measure width of quilt top through middle, including side borders. Trim remaining borders to match width. Sew borders to top and bottom edges of quilt, easing to fit as needed. Press seam allowances toward borders.

6. Appliqué Y pieces in place on top and bottom borders.

Quilting and Finishing

1. Layer backing, batting, and quilt top.

2. Quilt as desired. Quilt shown is outline-quilted.

3. Make 10½ yards of bias or straight-grain binding from reserved fabric. Bind quilt edges.

Color Variations

Your favorite fabrics may run to pastels or primaries, rather than the rich earthy hues that Annette Anderson used. These suggestions are food for thought.

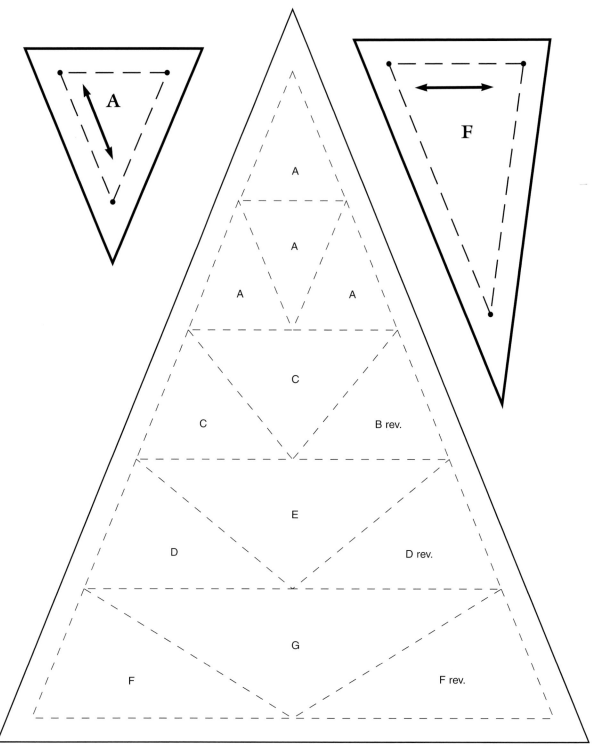

Paper Foundation Piecing Pattern

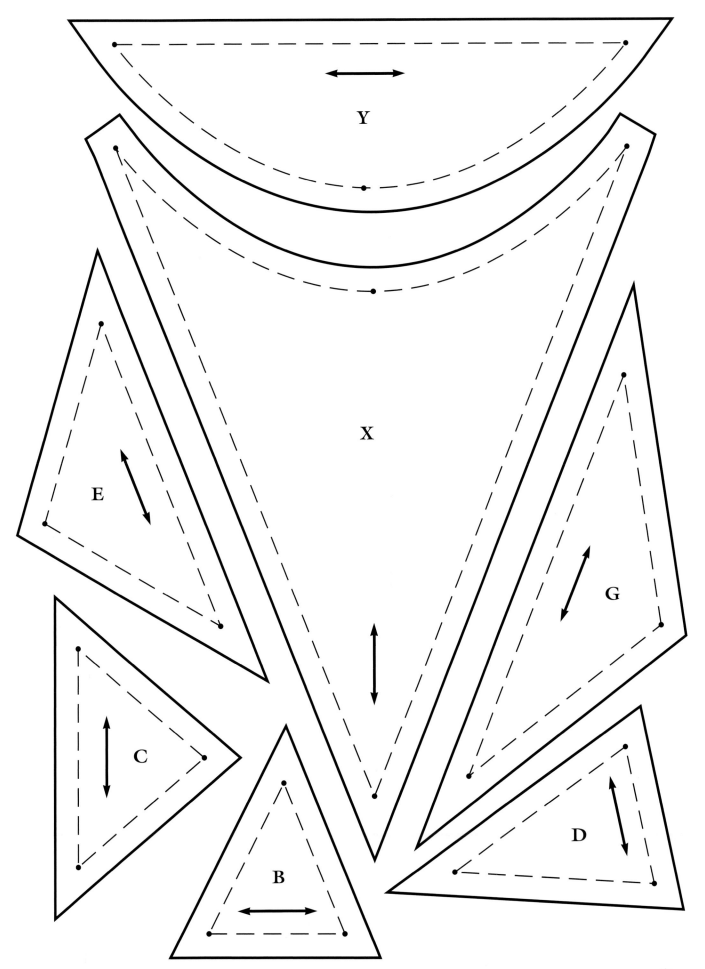

Y

X

E

G

C

B

D

Connie J. Nordstrom
Farmington, New Mexico

*W*hen Connie Nordstrom couldn't find an appropriate ready-made bedspread for an antique oak bed, she decided to make one. The quilt she made in 1983 had polyester fabric, thick batting, and erratic quilting stitches, but Connie was hooked.

In the early 1990s, Connie developed a passion for quilt history. "I became consumed with the origins of styles and

"I am so thankful for today's reproduction fabrics."

designs," she says. Today, Connie lectures on the influence of the industrial revolution on nineteenth-century quiltmaking, American appliqué, folk art quilts, and miniature quilts. She is currently researching the Pride of Iowa pattern to write a paper for the American Quilt Study Group.

"The quilts I make today are reproductions of nineteenth-century examples," Connie says. "I love connecting with early quiltmakers and their uninhibited creativity." Some of Connie's reproduction quilts are miniatures. She says, "Making miniatures is a way for me to make all the quilts that exist in my mind."

Connie is a member of the San Juan Quilters Guild and a bee called The Persian Pickle Club.

Fleur-de-lis
1999

This quilt was inspired by an antique quilt top, owned by Terry Clothier Thompson, that Connie Nordstrom saw about eight years ago.

The large center squares of this block provide an excellent opportunity to showcase large scale prints. In each block, the fabric for the appliquéd leaves coordinates with the center fabric.

For the border, Connie selected a brown-and-green printed swag design by Moda.

The quilt was assembled and quilted by machine. "I quilt by hand and by machine," Connie says. "Both are challenging and rewarding."

Fleur-de-lis was shown at the San Juan Quilters Guild's 2000 show.

Fleur-de-lis

Finished Size
Quilt: 87" x 99"
Blocks: 42 (10¾" x 10¾")

Materials*
42 (5¾") squares large print or
   stripe scrap fabrics
42 (10" x 14") coordinating
   small print scrap fabrics
4¼ yards muslin
2⅝ yards tan fabric for sashing
   and inner border
⅛ yard brown for sashing
   squares
3 yards print border fabric**
1 yard binding fabric
3 yards 104"-wide backing fabric
* *Note:* As in all scrap quilts,
   these yardages are recommendations. Use your own scraps
   and fabric placement as desired.
**Yardage is for lengthwise bor-
   der strips. If you need to cut
   cross-grain strips in order to
   accommodate border print, buy
   at least 2 yards.

Cutting
Make a template of leaf pattern
on page 55. Cut pieces in order
listed to make best use of yardage. Cut all strips cross-grain.
When possible, pieces are listed

Honeybee Block—Make 42.

in order needed, so you don't
have to cut everything all at once.
From each small print fabric
• 12 of Leaf Template.
From muslin
• 13 (11¼"-wide) strips. From
   these, cut 168 (3¼"x 11¼")
   strips for blocks.
From tan fabric
• 4 (2½" x 87") lengthwise
   strips for inner border.
• 71 (2¼" x 11¼") sashing
   strips.
From brown fabric
• 30 (2¼") sashing squares.
From outer border fabric
• 4 (6" x 106") lengthwise strips
   or 12 (6" x 43") cross-grain
   strips.

Block Assembly
1. For each block, choose 4
muslin strips, 1 (5¾") center
square, and 1 set of 12 leaves.
2. Fold each muslin strip in half
and crease to mark center. Mark
center on each edge of square in
same manner. Matching center
points, stitch a muslin strip onto
each side of square, starting and
stopping each seam ¼" from
edge of square. Miter corners.
Block should be 11¼" square.
3. Turn under seam allowance
on each leaf. Center 1 leaf over
each mitered seam, with bottom
point of leaf slightly above corner of center square. Pin 2 more
leaves on either side of each corner leaf. When satisfied with

placement, appliqué leaves in place to complete block.

4. Make 42 blocks.

Quilt Assembly

1. Referring to photograph, lay out blocks in 7 horizontal rows, with 6 blocks in each row. Place sashing strips between blocks. Arrange blocks to achieve a nice balance of color and pattern.

2. When satisfied with placement of blocks, join blocks and sashing in each row. Press seam allowances toward sashing strips.

3. Lay out block rows. Between block rows, lay out remaining sashing strips and sashing squares in horizontal rows, with 6 strips and 5 squares alternating in each row. Join sashing and squares in each sashing row. Press seam allowances toward sashing strips.

4. Referring to photograph, join all rows.

Borders

1. Measure length of quilt top through middle of pieced section. Trim 2 inner border strips to match quilt length.

2. Sew borders to quilt sides, easing to fit as needed. Press seam allowances toward borders.

3. Measure width of quilt top through middle, including side borders. Trim remaining inner borders to match width. Sew borders to top and bottom edges of quilt, easing to fit as needed. Press.

4. Mark center on each edge of quilt and each outer border strip. Matching centers, sew borders to quilt, starting and stopping each seam ¼" from corner. Miter border corners.

Quilting and Finishing

1. Layer backing, batting, and quilt top.

2. Quilt as desired. Quilt shown is outline-quilted with echo-quilting around appliqués and a clamshell pattern quilted in sashing. Fleur-de-lis Quilting Pattern for block center is below.

3. Make 10⅝ yards of bias or straight-grain binding from reserved strips. Bind quilt edges.

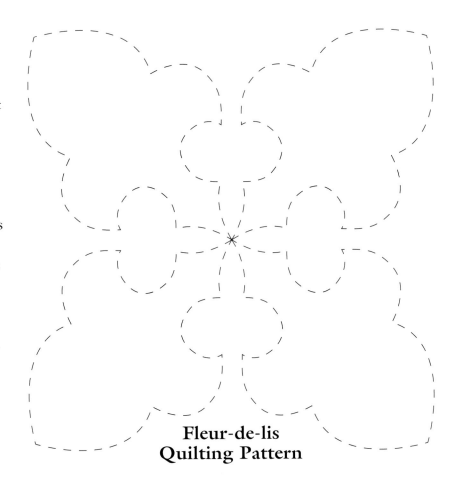

**Fleur-de-lis
Quilting Pattern**

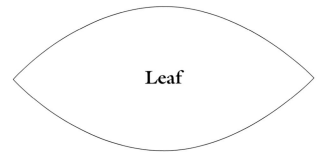

Leaf

Billie Tolmach
Mount Airy, Maryland

*G*uided by generations of family quilters, Billie Tolmach used to make traditional quilts in the traditional manner. Then, in 1991, a quiltmakers' trip to Japan changed Billie's outlook, her design sense, and her quilts.

"The experience was a milestone," Billie says of classes she took with quilters in Kyoto and Tokyo. "Everything I encountered there influenced what I did from then on."

Even when working with traditional design concepts, Billie sees fabrics, color, and technique in a different light now. In the 10 years since her Japan experience, her quilts have acquired a more contemporary look and include techniques such as machine quilting.

Billie is a member of Kaleidoscope and Milltown Quilters Guild, as well as Fiber Artists of Baltimore.

Lacquer Luster
1999

The high-gloss blacks and reds of Asian lacquerware inspired Billie Tolmach's fabric choices for this graphic interpretation of the classic Snowball block.

Lacquer Luster is based on a quilt by Judy Hopkins published in *101 Fabulous Rotary-Cut Quilts* (with permission, Martingale & Company/That Patchwork Place). Billie put her own spin on the block and created an original border design.

In 2000, *Lacquer Luster* was shown at Pacific International Quilt Festival, Quilters' Heritage Celebration, the Pennsylvania National Quilt Extravaganza, the National Quilting Association show, and the Delaware Valley Quilt Show, where it won an honorable mention.

Lacquer Luster

Finished Size

Quilt: 75" x 75"

Blocks: 100 (7½" x 7½")

Materials

13 (18" x 22") fat quarters assorted red fabrics

4 (½-yard) pieces black solid fabrics for border blocks (try brushed or polished cottons for visual contrast)

½ yard *each* white print and black solid for accent triangles

⅜ yard *each* black dot and white solid for border accent

1 yard binding fabric

4¾ yards backing fabric

Cutting

From red fabrics

• 26 (8" x 22") pieces. From these and remaining 2" x 22" strips, cut 8" strips, varying widths from 1¼" to 2½". Number of strips needed will vary, depending on widths cut.

From black fabrics

• 8 (8" x 42") strips. From these, cut 8" strips, varying widths from 1¼" to 2½".

From white print fabric and black solid fabric

• 6 (2¼"-wide) strips each. From these, cut 98 (2¼") squares of *each* fabric.

From black dot and white fabrics

• 4 (2¼"-wide) strips each. From these, cut 64 (2¼") squares of *each* fabric.

Block 1—Make 1.

Block 2—Make 3.

Block 3—Make 3.

Block 4—Make 1.

Block 5—Make 3.

Block 6—Make 18.

Block 7—Make 18.

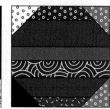

Block 8—Make 3.

Block 9—Make 3.

Block 10—Make 3.

Block 11—Make 1.

Block 12—Make 3.

Block 13—Make 3.

Block 14—Make 1.

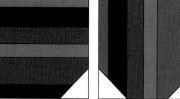

Block 15—Make 2.

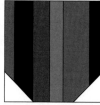

Block 16—Make 8.

Block 17—Make 7.

Block 18—Make 1.

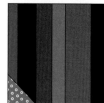

Block 19—Make 2.

Block 20—Make 8.

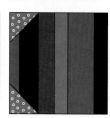

Block 21—Make 7.

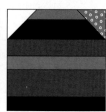

Block 22—Make 1.

❖QUILT SMART❖

Diagonal-Corners Quick-Piecing Method

The diagonal-corners technique turns squares into sewn triangles with just a stitch and a snip. This method is especially helpful when the corner triangle is very small, because it's easier to handle a square than a small triangle. And by sewing squares to squares, you don't have to guess where seam allowances match, which can be difficult with triangles.

1. A seam guide helps you sew diagonal lines without having to mark the fabric. Draw a line on graph paper. Place the paper on the sewing machine throatplate; lower needle onto line *(Photo A)*. (Remove presser foot if necessary to see what you're doing.) Use a ruler or a T-square to verify that line is parallel to needle or edges of throatplate. Tape paper in place. Trim paper as needed to clear needle and feed dogs.

2. Match small corner square to 1 corner of the base fabric, right sides facing. Align top tip of the small square with the needle and the bottom tip with seam guide. Stitch a seam from tip to tip, keeping bottom tip of small square in line with seam guide *(Photo B)*.
3. Press corner square in half at seam *(Photo C)*.
4. Trim seam allowance to ¼" *(Photo D)*.

Repeat procedure as needed to add a diagonal corner to 2, 3, or 4 corners of base fabric.

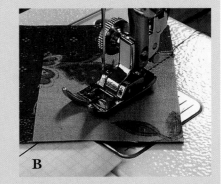

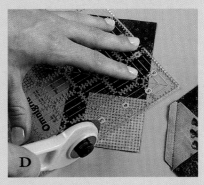

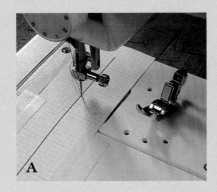

Block Assembly

There are 14 variations of corner treatments for the red blocks and 8 corner variations for black blocks, but the basic block is always the same. We recommend that you make all 64 red blocks and 36 black blocks; then add corner treatments.
1. For each block, select 4 or 5 strips of different fabrics and varying widths. Join strips lengthwise. Use a square ruler and rotary cutter to trim each completed block to 8" square.

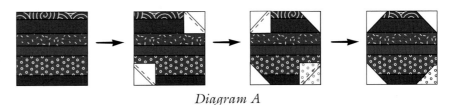

Diagram A

Make 64 red blocks and 36 black blocks.
2. See Quilt Smart above for step-by-step instructions for diagonal-corner quick-piecing technique. For Block 1, use diagonal-corner method to sew contrasting corners on 1 block as shown *(Diagram A)*. Note that

block seams are horizontal and that 3 corners are white solid and bottom right corner is white print fabric. Press.
3. Sew corners on all blocks, referring to block diagrams at left. Carefully note whether block seams are horizontal or vertical before adding corners.

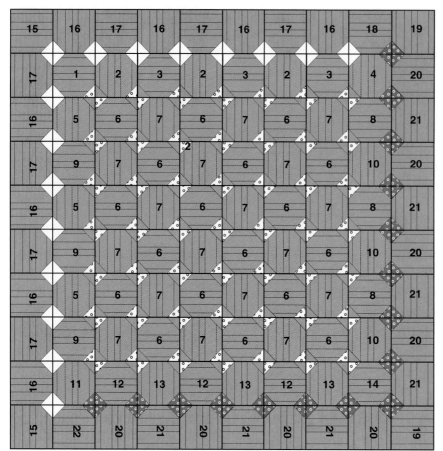

Quilt Assembly Diagram

Quilt Assembly

1. Referring to photo and *Quilt Assembly Diagram*, lay out red blocks in 8 horizontal rows with 8 blocks in each row. Note that direction of block seams alternates from horizontal to vertical. Plain white corners are at top and left edges; black dot corners are at right and bottom edges.

2. When satisifed with placement of blocks, join blocks in each row. Press all joining seam allowances toward blocks with vertical seams. Then join rows.

3. Lay assembled rows on floor; then lay out black blocks around outside edges.

4. When satisfied with layout, join blocks 16–18 for top border and blocks 20–22 for bottom border. Press seam allowances

---

Color Variations

This block is easy to sew, and it can be appealing in any color scheme. Here are some ideas to take to your scrap bag.

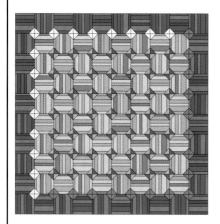
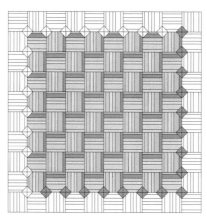
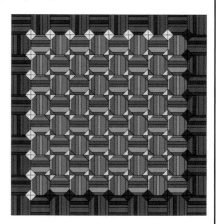

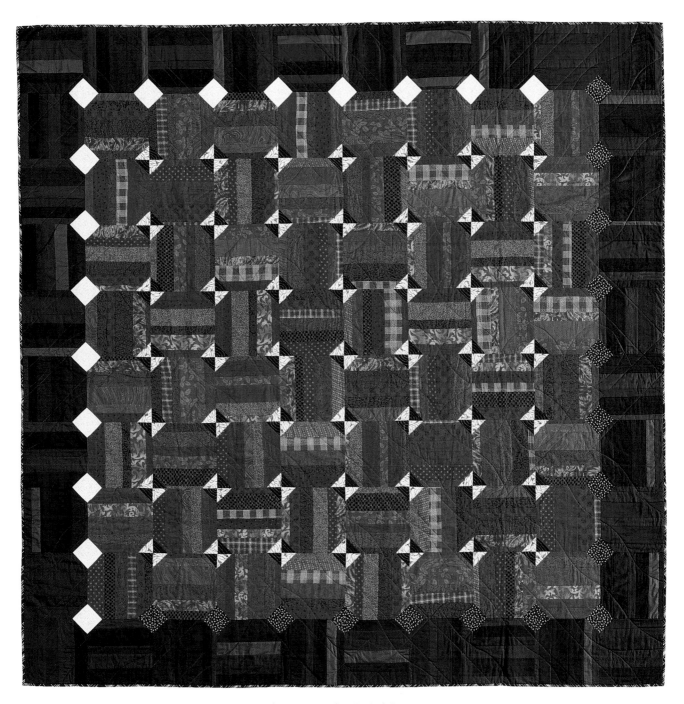

toward blocks 16 and 20. Sew borders to top and bottom edges of quilt.

5. Join remaining blocks for side borders. Press seam allowances toward blocks 17 and 21. Sew borders to quilt sides.

Quilting and Finishing

1. Assemble backing. Layer backing, batting, and quilt top.

2. Quilt as desired. Quilt shown is machine-quilted in an overall pattern of diagonal waves.

3. Make 8⅝ yards of bias or straight-grain binding from reserved fabric. Bind quilt edges.

Patricia Nicoll
Santa Maria, California

*I*n the mid-1980s, Pat Nicoll decided quilting wasn't for her. Her first quilt wasn't successful and, as much as she loved and admired quilts, they were just too hard to make. "I didn't know anyone who quilted or ever saw anyone quilt," Pat recalls. Then, in 1988, a local quilt shop opened, offering classes that changed everything for Pat.

"I learned so much!" she says, and this mother of four young boys started turning out at least one quilt a year. Then Pat joined the Santa Maria Valley Quilt Guild. "Here were people who love quilting as much as I do," she says. "The show-and-tell is always so inspiring."

"I never dreamed quilting would be such a blessing in my life."

Quilting helps Pat relax from the pressures of running a family business and raising a family. Workshops and guild challenges "help me grow as a quilter," Pat says. "I feel like I've only begun—there are so many quilts in my head, waiting to be made."

After such a rocky start as a quiltmaker, Pat was particularly interested in her mother's discovery of a 1956 letter written by Pat's great-grandmother who, at the age of 94, described a doll quilt she was making. It turns out there was a gene for quilting in the family, after all.

Diana's Rose
2000

Pat Nicoll likes her guild's challenges because they make her try things she might not otherwise do. *Diana's Rose* is a case in point.

The challenge called for each quilter to make a large traditional quilt, using the "Rose for Diana" fabric made by Rose & Hubble. Proceeds from the fabric purchase were donated to the Diana Princess of Wales Memorial Fund. Pat's problem was that she didn't care much for the royal blue fabric with large white roses.

After months of searching for the perfect design, Pat picked up a 1998 issue of *Quilter's Newsletter Magazine* and found this design by Charlotte Huber of Ferguson, Missouri (reprinted with permission). Pat altered the set and chose fabrics to coordinate with the challenge fabric, which she decided to use by centering a rose motif in the base piece of each block.

Diana's Rose won first-place ribbons at the Beauty of Traditional Quilt Show in Santa Maria in 2000 and Road to California in January 2001. In 2000, it was also Best of Show at the California State Fair and won a second-place ribbon at Pacific International Quilt Festival.

Diana's Rose

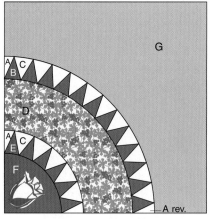

Block 1—Make 20.

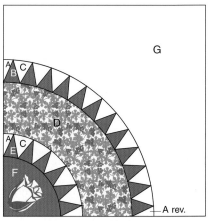

Block 2—Make 16.

Finished Size
Quilt: 81½" x 81½"
Blocks: 36 (9¼" x 9¼")

Materials
3¾ yards muslin
1¼ yards royal blue solid fabric
¼ yard royal blue rose fabric*
1¼ yards blue/green large print
     fabric
3¼ yards light blue fabric
1¼ yards green tone-on-tone
     fabric
¾ yard blue/green small print
     fabric
Scraps gray-green leaf prints or
     4 (9" x 22") fat eighths
5 yards backing fabric
*Note: Additional fabric may be
required to center a motif as in
quilt shown.

Cutting
Makes templates of patterns A–N
on pages 67–69. Cut all strips
cross-grain unless otherwise speci-
fied. Cut pieces in order listed to
make best use of yardage. When
possible, pieces are listed in
order needed, so you don't have
to cut everything all at once.
From muslin
- 4 (10"-wide) strips. From
  these, cut 16 of Template G.
- 9 (5½"-wide) strips. From
  these, cut 9 (5½" x 24") and
  18 (5½" x 9¾") sashing strips.
- 576 of Template C (16 for
  each block).
- 72 of Template A (2 for each
  block).
- 72 of Template A reversed (2
  for each block).
From royal blue solid fabric
- 432 of Template B (12 for

each block).
- 216 of Template E (6 for each
  block).
- 9 of Template M.
From royal blue rose fabric
- 36 of Template F. Center rose
  motif, if desired.
From large print fabric
- 36 of Template D.
From light blue fabric
- 4 (5¼" x 88") lengthwise
  strips for border.
- 20 of Template G.
- 9 of Template N.
From green tone-on-tone fabric
- 1 (6¾"-wide) strip for vines.
- 1 (30") square for bias binding.
- 36 of Template J.
From small print fabric
- 8 (1"-wide) inner border strips.
- 36 (2½") squares for K buds.
- 9 of Template L.
From gray-green scraps
- 144 of Template I (leaves).

Block Assembly
Instructions are for traditional
piecing. If you prefer paper piecing, use Full-size Placement
Guide (page 68) to make paper
foundations.
1. For 1 block, select 2 each of A
and A reversed, 12 B, 16 C,
1 D, 6 E, and 1 F.

2. Starting with outer arc, join
12 Bs and 11 Cs (*Block Assembly
Diagram*). (If you prefer, you
can assemble block in opposite
direction, from F corner piece to
outer arc.) Add A and A reversed
at row ends. Compare assembled
row with Full-size Placement
Guide; make any needed adjust-
ments. Press all seam allowances
in 1 direction.
3. Join D to bottom of ABC arc.
(See Quilt Smart, page 27, for
tips on sewing a curved seam.)
Press seam allowance toward D.
4. Assemble inner arc with 6 Es,
5 Cs, A, and A reversed. Join arc
to bottom of D. Check piecing
against placement guide.
5. Sew F to bottom of inner arc.
6. Complete 36 arc units.

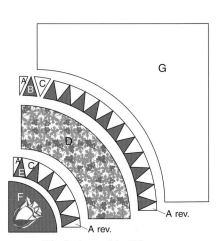

Block Assembly Diagram

7. Add blue Gs to 20 arc units for Block 1. Add muslin Gs to 16 units for Block 2. Press seam allowances toward Gs.

Quilt Assembly

1. Lay out blocks in 6 horizontal rows with 6 blocks in each row, placing blue and muslin blocks as shown *(Quilt Assembly Diagram)*. Place 24"-long sashing strips horizontally between alternate block rows; place short sashing strips vertically between block pairs. When satisfied with layout, join blocks and sashing strips in 4-block units as shown.

2. To cut bias for vines (H), cut a 6¾" right triangle off 1 corner of 6¾" green strip *(Diagram A)*. Measuring from diagonal (bias) cut edge, cut 36 (¾"-wide) bias strips, each about 9½" long.

3. With wrong sides facing, fold each bias strip in thirds to measure ¼" wide. Press.

4. Center L, M, and N on each horizontal sashing strip and pin. Pin H vines in place at top, bottom, left, and right of L. Pin 4 I leaves and 1 J piece on each vine as shown.

5. For rosebuds (K), fold 2½" squares in half, wrong sides facing *(Diagram B)*. Fold right corner into center *(Diagram C)*. Then fold left corner over to align with first fold, making a triangle with jagged ends *(Diagram D)*. Baste edges in place, if desired. Slip raw edges of a folded rosebud under turned edge of each J piece and pin.

6. When satisfied with placement of all appliqué pieces, stitch pieces in place in alphabetical order. Stitch J over raw edges of

rosebud, leaving folded edges of bud free *(Diagram E)*. Press completed appliqué.

7. Join 4-block units in 3 rows. Join rows.

Borders

1. Join 1"-wide print strips end-to-end in pairs to get a border strip for each quilt side.

2. Matching centers, sew a narrow border to each light blue border to get 1 (2-strip) unit for each quilt side.

Quilt Assembly Diagram

Diagram A

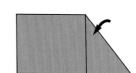

Diagram B

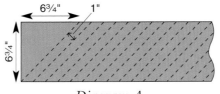

Diagram C

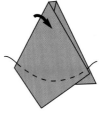

Diagram D

Diagram E

3. Matching centers, sew border units to quilt sides. Miter border corners. Press seam allowances toward borders.

Quilting and Finishing

1. Assemble backing. Layer backing, batting, and quilt top.
2. Quilt as desired. Quilt shown is outline-quilted. See Pattern G for feather design quilted in each block. Quilt shown also has a diagonal grid of ¾" squares quilted in sashing and a feather vine quilted in outer border.
3. Make 9⅜ yards of bias binding from reserved green square. Bind quilt edges.

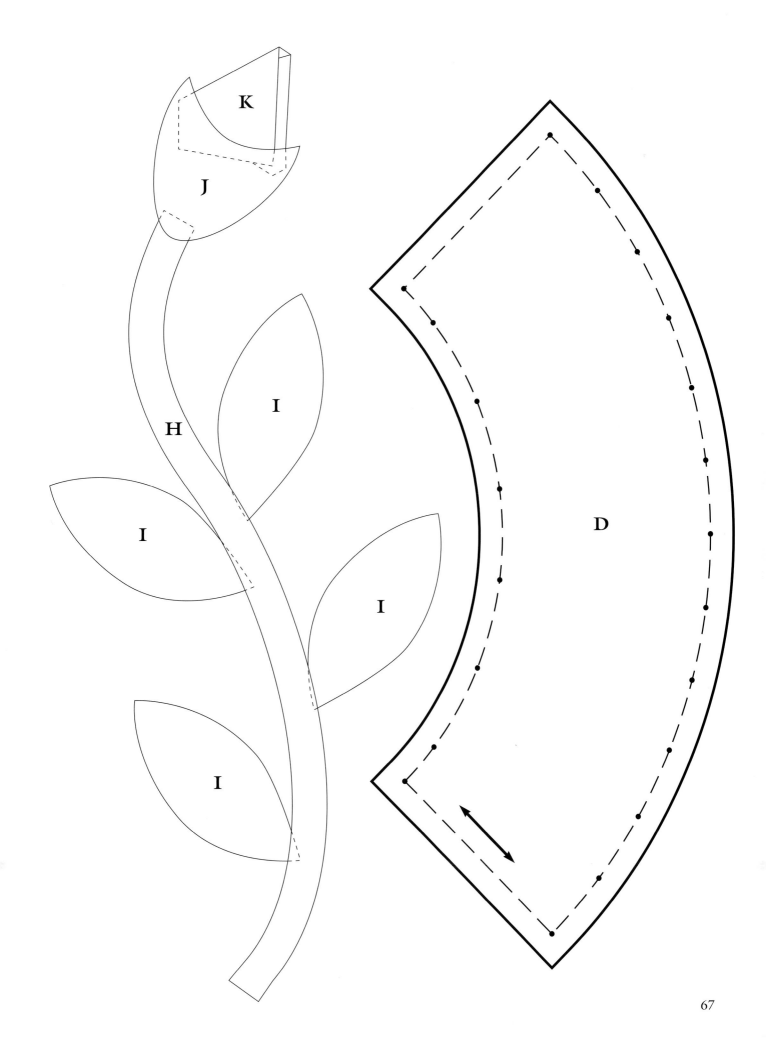

K

J

H

I

I

I

I

D

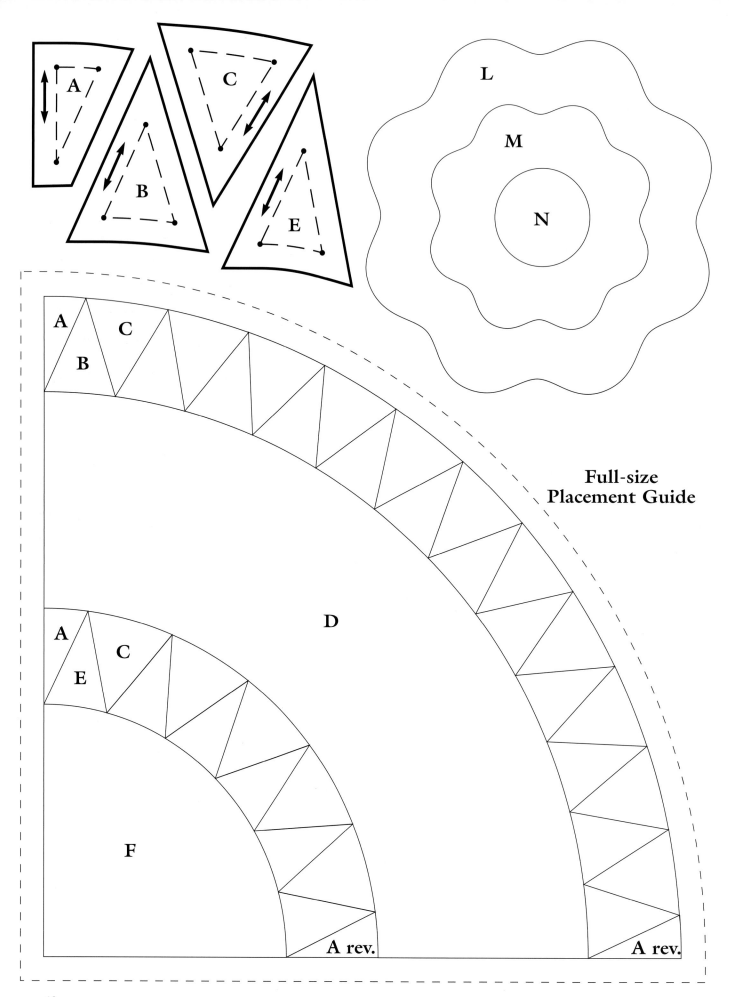

A

C

B

E

L

M

N

Full-size
Placement Guide

A
C
B

A
C
E

D

F

A rev.

A rev.

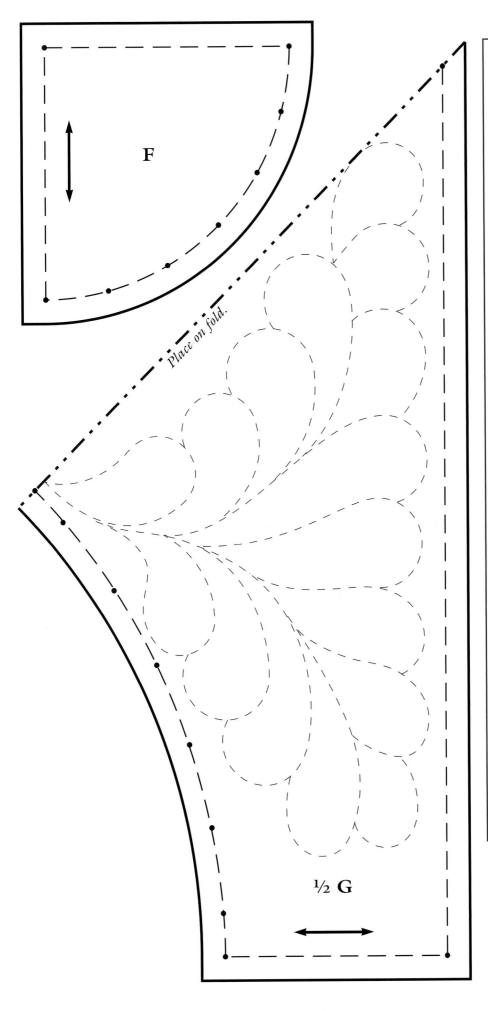

F

Place on fold.

½ G

Color Variations

Roses come in many colors, so how does your garden grow? These varied interpretations are examples of the different paths you can take to creating beautiful patchwork.

Dee Doebler
Batesburg, South Carolina

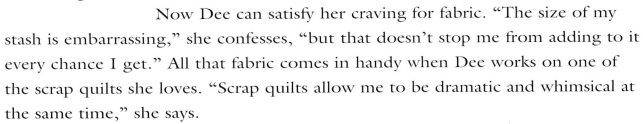

When you're a woman who's a professional pipe welder, working on something soft and bright and comforting is a nice change of pace. That's part of the reason Dee Doebler started making quilts.

That was more than 20 years ago, when there were few books or tools available and no shop to help or to teach classes. It took Dee five years to complete her first quilt. But when she retired about 10 years ago, she could indulge this new-found pleasure.

"The size of my stash is embarrassing."

Now Dee can satisfy her craving for fabric. "The size of my stash is embarrassing," she confesses, "but that doesn't stop me from adding to it every chance I get." All that fabric comes in handy when Dee works on one of the scrap quilts she loves. "Scrap quilts allow me to be dramatic and whimsical at the same time," she says.

Dee describes her style as eclectic. "I like to try everything at least once," she says. "Giving myself permission to machine quilt is the best thing I ever did—it set me free."

Teaching and sharing her work is Dee's greatest pleasure. She says, "Success for me is seeing folks reach out to touch my quilts and seeing their smiles."

Dee is a member of Fringe Sisters, Logan Lap Quilters and Devine Quilters of Columbia, Quilters of South Carolina, and the Charlotte (North Carolina) Quilters Guild.

Reflections
2000

"Movement and color have always been my inspiration," says Dee Doebler, and this quilt certainly moves.

Dee started with an old pattern called Swirl. Then she experimented with color, value, and mirror-imaging to produce the design. Like the Chinese yin-yang symbol, it relies on the contrast of light and dark to create a whole.

Reflections was the finalist for South Carolina at the American Quilter's Society's 2000 Quilt Exposition in Nashville. It also won a second-place ribbon for innovative appliqué at the 2000 International Quilt Festival in Houston.

Reflections

Finished Size
Quilt: 67½" x 81"
Blocks: 80 (6¾" x 6¾")

Materials*
28 (18" x 22") fat quarters light
    print scrap fabrics
22 (18" x 22") fat quarters dark
    print scrap fabrics
⅞ yard binding fabric
4½ yards backing fabric
Freezer paper
80 (8") squares foundation paper
    (see Quilt Smart below)
*Note: As in all scrap quilts,
these yardages are recommendations. Use your own scraps and
fabric placement as desired.

❖ QUILT ❖ SMART
Paper Foundations
You can use any kind of
paper for a foundation—
newsprint, tracing paper,
paper towels—as long as it is
sturdy enough to hold up
through assembly of the
block, yet easily torn away
from the seam without
pulling out the stitches.

Dee Doebler recommends
banquet paper, a textured
paper usually available at
party supply stores. (It's
often used as a table covering
at group suppers.) Banquet
paper is sold in 40"-wide
rolls and is much less expen-
sive to buy in quantity than
other types of lightweight
paper. And, Dee says, it tears
easily.

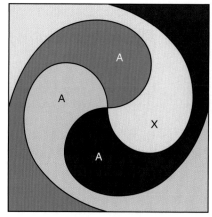
Block 1—Make 24.

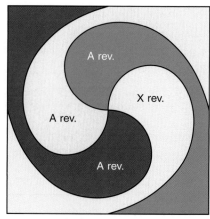
Block 2—Make 24.

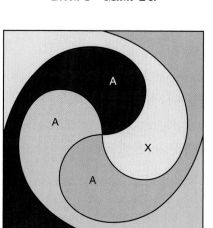
Block 3—Make 16.

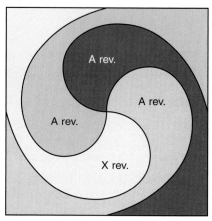
Block 4—Make 16.

Cutting
Make templates of patterns X, A,
and B on page 75. Cut pieces in
order listed to make best use of
yardage. When possible, pieces
are listed in order needed, so
you don't have to cut everything
all at once.

Note: Trace Templates A and
X on *wrong* side of scrap fabrics.
From light fabrics
- 40 of Template X (1 each for
  Blocks 1 and 3).
- 40 of Template X reversed (1
  each for Blocks 2 and 4).
- 56 of Template A (1 for each
  Block 1 and 2 for each Block 3).
- 56 of Template A reversed (1
  for each Block 2 and 2 for
  each Block 4).
- 40 (1½" x 18") strips for
  pieced border.

From dark fabrics
- 64 of Template A (2 for
  each Block 1 and 1 for each
  Block 3).
- 64 of Template A reversed
  (2 for each Block 2 and 1 for
  each Block 4).
- 40 (1½" x 18") strips for
  pieced border.
- 20 (3½" x 18") strips of dark-
  est fabrics for outer border.

From freezer paper
Trace template onto paper (dull)
side of freezer paper.
- 120 of Template B (3 each for
  Blocks 1 and 3).
- 120 of Template B reversed (3
  each for Blocks 2 and 4).

Block Assembly

1. For each Block 1, select 1 foundation square, 1 X piece, 1 light A piece, 2 dark A pieces, and 3 B paper pieces.

2. Place a paper piece B on wrong side of 1 dark A piece, aligning corners *(Diagram A)*. Paper should be shiny side up. Clip outside curve of fabric piece as needed. Use tip of a hot, dry iron to press fabric seam allowance onto paper (see ironing tip at right). Then clip and press inside curve. *Keep corners of fabric and paper aligned at all times.* Prepare light A piece in same manner. For remaining dark A, clip and press outside curve only.

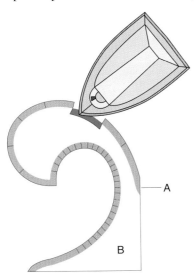

Diagram A

❖ QUILT SMART ❖
Ironing Tip

Use an iron with as sharp a point as you can find. Also, use as hard an ironing surface as possible. You want to apply pressure to these pieces, and you don't want the effort to get lost in a spongy pad. Be sure to keep the iron only on the fabric, as a hot iron will melt the waxy surface of the paper and make a mess on your iron. It's a good idea to have some iron cleaning solution handy.

3. Place X piece face up on lower left corner of foundation square, matching corners precisely *(Diagram B)*.

4. Pin dark A piece (with only 1 side pressed) in lower right corner, overlapping first piece, and matching corners of fabric and foundation *(Diagram C)*. Starting at outside edge, appliqué

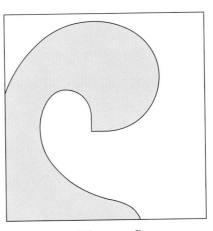

Diagram B

outside curve of dark piece by hand or by machine. Stitch to center of block. Remove freezer paper from A. Press. *Note:* For machine appliqué, use an open-toed embroidery foot *(Diagram D)*. Select a blind-hem stitch and set machine to a short stitch length and narrow width, just enough to catch a few threads of piece being appliquéd.

5. Lay light A in upper right corner of foundation, matching corners and overlapping previous pieces *(Diagram E)*. Appliqué outside curve. Remove freezer paper.

6. Lay remaining dark piece (with both curves pressed) in upper left corner, matching corners. Stitch from outside edge of outside curve to center, pivot, and sew inside curve from center

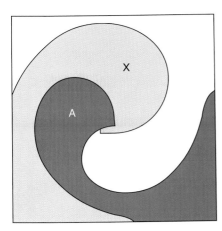

Diagram C

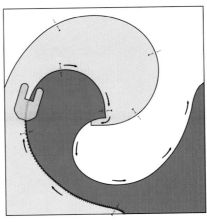

Diagram D

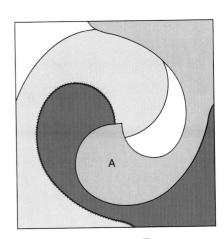

Diagram E

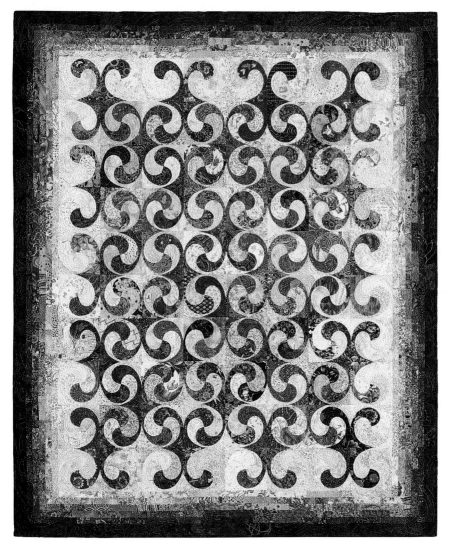

to outer edge. (Legs of stitched pieces will not always be same width.) Remove freezer paper.

7. Make 24 of Block 1. Make 16 of Block 3 in same manner, using 1 X, 1 dark A, and 2 light As in each block as shown.

8. Use X reversed and A reversed pieces to make 24 of Block 2 as shown. Make 16 of Block 4 in same manner, using 1 X reversed, 1 dark A reversed, and 2 light As reversed in each block as shown.

9. Carefully remove foundation paper from back of each block and press. Measuring out from center of block, square and trim each block to 7¼" square.

Quilt Assembly

1. Referring to photograph, lay out 8 blocks for Row 1, starting with a Block 4 and alternating blocks 3 and 4, ending with a Block 3.

2. For rows 2, 4, 6, and 8, start with a Block 3 and then alternate blocks 2 and 1, ending with a Block 4.

3. For rows 3, 5, and 7, start with a Block 4 and then alternate blocks 1 and 2, ending with a Block 3.

4. Row 10 is Row 1 in reverse. Start with a Block 3 and alternate blocks 4 and 3, ending with a Block 4.

5. When satisfied with placement of blocks, join blocks in each row. Press.

6. Join rows.

Borders

1. Sort 1½"-wide strips into 4 value groups: lightest, light, medium, and dark.

2. From lightest strips, cut 68 segments 4¼"–4½" long. Join 18 segments end-to-end for each side border and 15 segments end-to-end each for top and bottom borders.

3. Measure length of quilt top through middle of pieced section. Trim side border strips to match quilt length. Sew borders to quilt sides, easing to fit as needed. Press seam allowances toward borders.

4. Measure width of quilt top through middle, including side borders. Trim top and bottom borders to match width. Sew borders to top and bottom edges of quilt, easing to fit as needed. Press seam allowances toward borders.

5. Cut 70 (4¼"–4½"-long) segments from light strips for second border. Join 19 segments end-to-end for side borders and 15 segments each for top and bottom borders. Join borders to quilt top in same manner as for first border.

6. From medium strips, cut 74 segments, 20 for each side border and 17 each for top and bottom borders. Assemble and join borders to quilt as before.

7. From dark strips, cut 76 segments. Join 21 segments for each side border and 17 each for top and bottom borders. Assemble and join borders to quilt top.

8. From 3"-wide dark strips, cut 78 (4¼"-long) segments. Join 21 segments for each side border and 18 segments each for top and bottom border. Join borders to quilt top. Press seam allowances toward borders.

Quilting and Finishing

1. Assemble backing. Layer backing, batting, and quilt top.

2. Quilt as desired. Quilt shown is machine-quilted with an all-over pattern.

3. Make 8½ yards of bias or straight-grain binding from reserved fabric. Bind quilt edges.

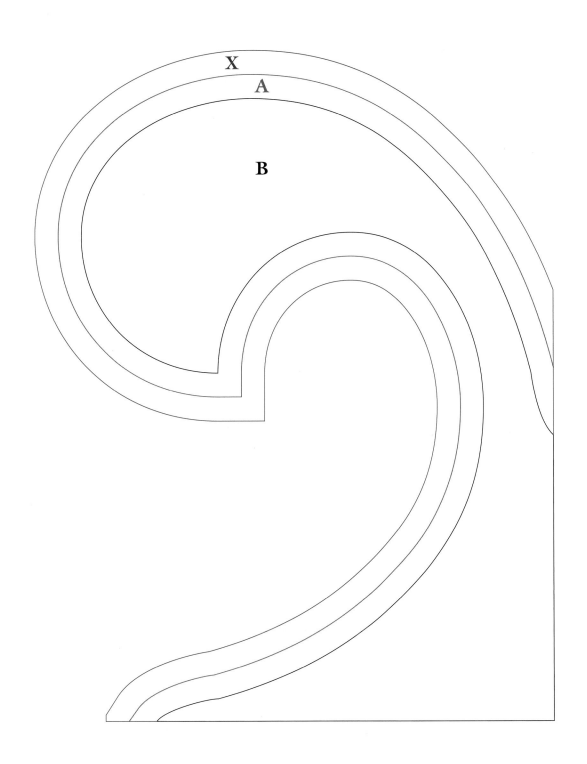

Linda D. Greuter
Houston, Texas

Twenty years ago, a quilt shop opened in Linda Greuter's neighborhood and she thought taking a quilting class might be fun. That's when she discovered what she calls "this fabric thing."

A fourth-generation quiltmaker, it's only natural that Linda would fall in love with fabric. She says, "When I'm gone, maybe my children and grandchildren will have finished quilts to enjoy instead of stacks and stacks of fabric."

Toward that end, Linda uses long airplane trips and time away to work on "UFOs," unfinished projects. She spends half the year in Houston and half in Indonesia with her husband. While she's away, Houston friends send Linda supplies and instructions so she can continue to share in block exchanges.

Linda is a member of the Bay Area Quilt Guild and the Scrap Bee.

Warm Cabin Nights
1998

Houston's Scrap Bee is a very productive group—they do a lot of block exchanges. To make *Warm Cabin Nights,* Linda Greuter came up with a creative set that combined Log Cabin and Fan blocks from these exchanges.

The arrangement of blocks that forms the center star was inspired by a Delectable Mountains set. Linda surrounded the center medallion with concentric frames of Fan blocks and more Log Cabin blocks.

The up-and-down placement of the fans' curves creates an undulating wave that provides relief from the hard lines and angles of the Log Cabin blocks.

Warm Cabin Nights

Finished Size

Quilt: 97½" x 97½"
Blocks: 108 (7½" x 7½")

Materials*

32 (18" x 22") fat quarters
    medium/dark scrap fabrics
10 (18" x 22") fat quarters light
    scrap fabrics
¼ yard *each* of 5 light fabrics
⅝ yard *each* of 3 light fabrics
¼ yard dark cranberry print
    fabric
⅛ yard *each* of 2 red fabrics
⅜ yard navy border fabric
3 yards 104"-wide backing
* *Note:* As in all scrap quilts,
these yardages are recommendations. Use your own scraps and
fabric placement as desired.

Cutting

Make templates of patterns X, Y,
and Z on page 81. Pieces are listed in order needed, so you don't
have to cut everything at once.
From medium/dark fat quarters
- 24 (5" x 22") strips. From
  these, cut 288 of Template Z.
- 300 (1¼" x 22") strips.
From light fat quarters
- 144 (1¼" x 22") strips.
From each ¼ yard light fabric
- 5 of Template Y.
From ⅝ yard light fabrics
- 15 (8") squares. From these,
  cut 11 of Template Y. Set aside
  4 setting squares.
- 8 (12") squares. Cut 6 squares
  in quarters diagonally to get
  24 setting triangles. Cut 2
  squares in half diagonally for 4
  corner triangles.

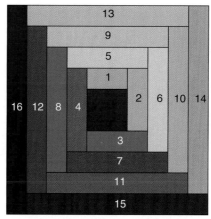

Log Cabin Block—Make 72.

- 4 (1¼" x 22") strips. Add
  these to light Log Cabin strips.
From cranberry fabric
- 1 (5¾" x 44") strip. From
  this, cut 4 (5¾" x 6½") pieces
  for border corners. From remainder, cut 6 of Template X
  and 8 (2") squares for Log
  Cabin blocks.
- 1 (2" x 44") strip. From this,
  cut 22 (2") squares for Log
  Cabin blocks.
- 2 (1¼" x 22") strips. Add
  these to dark Log Cabin strips.
From each red fabric
- 1 (2" x 44") strip. From this,
  cut 21 (2") squares for Log
  Cabin blocks.
- 15 of Template X.
From navy border fabric
- 8 (1½" x 44") strips.
- 4 (1¼" x 22") strips. Add
  these to dark Log Cabin strips.

Log Cabin Block Assembly

1. For each block, choose 1 (2")
red square, 8 (1¼" x 22") light
strips, and 8 dark strips.
2. With right sides facing, match
any light strip to 1 side of square
and stitch *(Diagram A)*. Trim
log even with bottom of square.
Press seam allowance toward log.

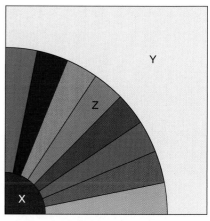

Fan Block—Make 36.

3. Turn unit so Log 1 is at top.
Match another light strip to next
edge of square and stitch *(Diagram B)*. Trim new log even
with bottom of unit. Press seam
allowance toward Log 2.
4. Turn unit so Log 2 is at top.
Match a dark strip to next edge
of square and stitch *(Diagram
C)*. Trim log even with bottom
of unit and press seam allowance
toward Log 3.

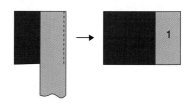

Diagram A

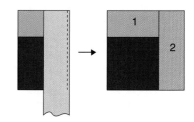

Diagram B

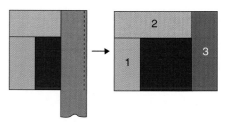

Diagram C

5. Continue adding logs in numerical order until you have 4 logs on each side of center square *(Block Diagram)*. Always press seam allowances toward newest log; then rotate unit to put it at top edge to add next log.

6. Make 72 Log Cabin blocks. Set aside remaining dark strips for pieced border and binding.

Fan Block Assembly

1. For each block, select 1 each of X and Y, and 8 assorted Zs.

2. Join Zs edge-to-edge to make a fan. Press all seam allowances in same direction.

3. Sew X and Y to raw edges of fan *(Fan Block Assembly Diagram)*. You can stitch this seam (see page 27 for tips on sewing curved seams), or you can turn under seam allowances on X and Y and appliqué them to the fan.

4. Make 36 Fan blocks.

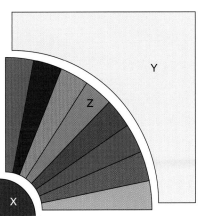

Fan Block Assembly Diagram

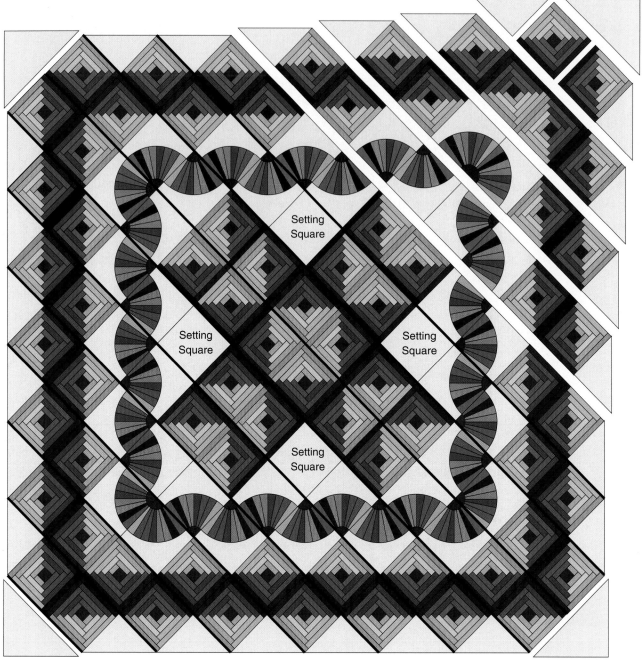

Quilt Assembly Diagram

Quilt Assembly

1. Lay out blocks in 14 diagonal rows *(Quilt Assembly Diagram)*. Insert setting squares at middle points of center star. Carefully check position of each block. Add setting triangles at row ends as shown.

2. When satisfied with placement of blocks, join blocks in each row. Return each assembled row to layout as you go and double-check position of each block.

3. Join rows.

4. Add corner triangles. If these triangles are slightly too big, just trim them to fit.

Borders

1. Join 2 navy strips end-to-end to get an inner border strip for each quilt edge.

2. Measure length of quilt top through middle of pieced section. Trim 2 inner border strips to match quilt length. Sew borders to quilt sides, easing to fit as needed. Press seam allowances toward borders.

3. Measure width of quilt top through middle, including side borders. Trim remaining inner borders to match width. Sew these to top and bottom edges of quilt, easing to fit as needed.

4. Cut 456 (1¼" x 5¾") pieces from remaining dark strips.

5. Join 113 strips edge-to-edge for top border. Referring to photo, sew border to top edge of quilt, easing to fit as needed. (If necessary, feel free to add or remove 1 or 2 pieces from border for a better fit.) Repeat for bottom border. Press seam allowances toward inner border.

6. Join 115 strips edge-to-edge for each side border. Sew cranberry corner pieces to ends of each row. Stitch borders to quilt sides, easing to fit as needed.

Quilting and Finishing

1. Layer backing, batting, and quilt top.

2. Quilt as desired. Quilt shown is outline-quilted.

3. Join varying lengths from remaining dark strips end-to-end to make 11⅛ yards (400") of straight-grain binding. Bind quilt edges.

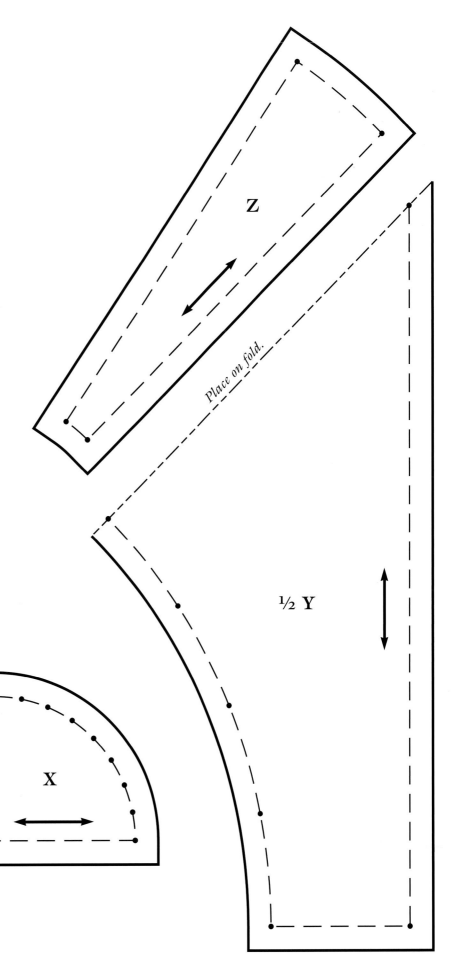

Z

Place on fold.

½ Y

X

Traditions in Quilting

Jenny's Flower Garden

Communion

Ohio Rose

Generations

That's Cool

Delectable Mountains

Elaine M. Nielson
Seward, Nebraska

When Elaine Nielson works with antique tops and blocks, she feels a link with quilters of the past.

Since taking up quilting seriously 10 years ago, Elaine has completed several projects using antique materials. But she's not tied to the traditional. She'll try anything new—different settings, a change in scale, embellishments, or some other unorthodox element. Some of her original designs are pictorial interpretations of a story.

Elaine combines creative writing, her other love, with quilting by adding quilt labels that tell a story or provide historical documentation for the quilt.

Elaine is a member of the Lincoln Quilter's Guild, the Blue Valley Quilt Guild, and the Nebraska State Quilt Guild. She says a small group, The Material Girls, "provides the best support, encouragement, and fun imaginable!"

Jenny's Flower Garden
1999

This classic quilt was made by two women, kindred spirits a generation apart.

The top was hand-pieced by Elizabeth Jenny Cobb (1872–1947) of St. Joseph, Missouri. After Jenny passed away, the top was stored by her cousin until 1991, when it was rescued from the trash bin by Elaine Nielsen's aunt.

Elaine removed a row of blocks from one end of the quilt and used these pieces to finish the incomplete border.

Elaine says, "This quilt is named in honor of the original piecemaker by one who is happy to complete it for her. Though our lives didn't overlap, we share the love of piecing and color and quilts."

Jenny's Flower Garden

Finished Size
Quilt: 82" x 82"
Blocks: 49 (10½" x 10½")

Materials*
17 (18" x 22") fat quarters
  print scrap fabrics
1 (9" x 22") fat eighth yellow
  solid fabric
1 yard pink solid fabric (includes
  binding)
1 yard green solid fabric
3¼ yards muslin
5 yards 44"-wide backing fabric
  or 2½ yards 90"-wide fabric
* *Note:* As in all scrap quilts,
these yardages are recommendations. Use your own scraps and
fabric placement as desired. Add
leftover border and setting fabrics to scraps, if desired.

Cutting
Instructions are for rotary cutting and quick piecing. When
possible, pieces are listed in
order needed, so you don't have
to cut everything all at once.
From scrap fabrics
• 150 (2" x 22") strips.
From yellow fabric
• 3 (2" x 22") strips.
From pink fabric
• 11 (2" x 22") strips.
• 8 (2½" x 42") strips for
  straight-grain binding.
From green fabric
• 25 (2" x 22") strips.
From muslin
• 37 (2" x 22") strips.
• 10 (5" x 22") strips.
• 5 (8" x 42") strips. From
  these, cut 24 (8") squares for
  Block 2.

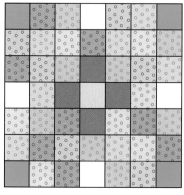

Block 1—Make 25.

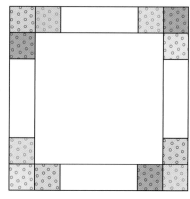

Block 2—Make 24.

Block Assembly
Note: In *Strip Set Diagrams,*
muslin, pink, yellow, and green
fabrics are shown in required
positions. All other fabrics are
random scrap fabrics of any color.
1. For Strip Set 1, select 2 green
strips, 1 muslin strip, and 4 scrap
strips. Join strips as shown (*Strip*

Set 1 Diagram). Make 5 of Strip
Set 1, using different scrap fabrics
in each. Press seam allowances
toward center (muslin) strip.
2. Rotary-cut 10 (2"-wide) segments from each of Strip Set 1
to get 50 segments for Block 1.
3. Join 7 scrap strips for each
Strip Set 2 (*Strip Set 2 Diagram*).

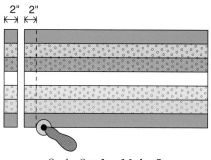

Strip Set 1—Make 5.

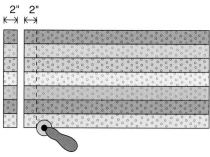

Strip Set 2—Make 5.

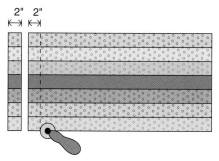

Strip Set 3—Make 5.

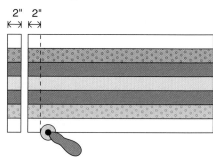

Strip Set 4—Make 3.

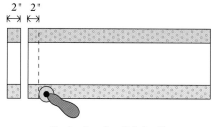

Strip Set 5—Make 5.

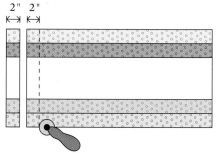

Strip Set 6—Make 5.

Press seam allowances toward center strip. Rotary-cut 50 (2"-wide) segments for Block 1.

4. For Strip Set 3, select 1 pink strip and 6 scrap strips. Make 5 of Strip Set 2 as shown *(Strip Set 3 Diagram)*. Press seam allowances toward center (pink) strip. Cut 50 (2"-wide) segments for Block 1.

5. For Strip Set 4, select 2 pink strips, 1 yellow strip, 2 muslin strips, and 2 scrap strips. Make 3 of Strip Set 4 as shown *(Strip Set 4 Diagram)*. Press seam allowances toward center (yellow) strip. Cut 25 (2"-wide) segments for Block 1.

6. For Block 1, select 2 segments from each of strip sets 1, 2, and 3, and 1 Set 4 segment. Join 7 segments as shown *(Block 1 Assembly Diagram)*, turning them as needed to get opposing seam allowances in adjacent rows. Make 25 of Block 1.

7. For Strip Set 5, sew 2 scrap strips to opposite sides of 1 (5"-wide) muslin strip as shown *(Strip Set 5 Diagram)*. Make 5 of Strip Set 5. Press seam allowances toward center (muslin) strip. Cut 48 (2"-wide) segments for Block 2.

8. For Strip Set 6, select 4 scrap strips and 1 (5"-wide) muslin

strip. Make 5 of Strip Set 6 as shown *(Strip Set 6 Diagram)*. Press seam allowances toward center (muslin) strip. Cut 48 (2"-wide) segments for Block 2.

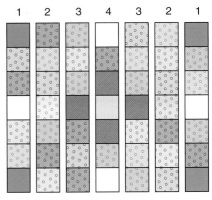

Block 1 Assembly Diagram

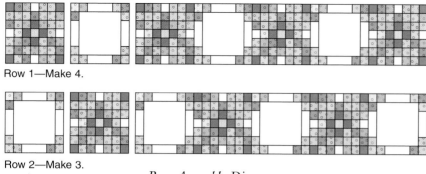

Row 1—Make 4.

Row 2—Make 3.

Row Assembly Diagram

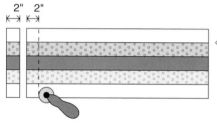

Strip Set 7—Make 13.

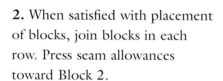

Border Diagram

9. For each Block 2, select 1 (8") muslin square and 2 segments from each of strip sets 5 and 6. Join Set 5 segments to square as shown *(Block 2 Assembly Diagram)*. Then add Set 6 segments to complete block. Make 24 of Block 2.

Quilt Assembly

1. Lay out blocks in 7 horizontal rows *(Row Assembly Diagram)*. Start odd-numbered rows (rows 1, 3, 5, and 7) with Block 1 and alternate blocks as shown. Start even-numbered rows (2, 4, and 6) with Block 2.

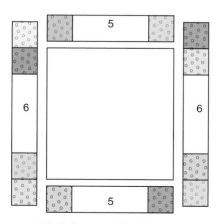

Block 2 Assembly Diagram

2. When satisfied with placement of blocks, join blocks in each row. Press seam allowances toward Block 2.

3. Referring to photo on page 87, join block rows.

Borders

1. For each Strip Set 7, select 2 muslin strips, 1 green strip, and 2 scrap strips. Make 13 of Strip Set 7 as shown *(Strip Set 7 Diagram)*. Press seam allowances toward center (green) strip. From these, rotary-cut 128 (2"-wide) segments for borders.

2. Join 32 segments in a row for each border *(Border Diagram)*. Match seam lines carefully, stepping down each adjacent segment so that top muslin square is opposite first scrap square of previous segment. Press borders.

3. Use an acrylic ruler and rotary cutter to trim muslin squares along both sides of pieced border strip. Be sure to leave ¼" seam allowance. (If you prefer, you can sew border seams first, and then trim excess fabric from seam.)

4. Sew borders to edges of quilt, easing to fit as needed. Press.

5. For 1 corner unit, cut 4 (2") green squares, 8 (2") muslin squares, and 8 (2") squares of scrap fabrics. Join squares in rows *(Corner Unit Diagram)*. Then join rows to complete unit. Make 4 corner units.

6. Sew straight edge of a corner unit to each corner of quilt. Trim muslin squares on each side, leaving ¼" seam allowance.

Quilting and Finishing

1. Assemble backing. Layer backing, batting, and quilt top.

2. Quilt as desired. Quilt shown is outline-quilted, and large roses are quilted in center of each Block 2. To find an appropriate quilting design for Block 2, look for a stencil design such as a feathered wreath or flower that has a diameter of about 6".

3. Make 9⅜ yards of straight-grain binding from reserved pink strips. Bind quilt edges.

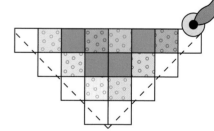

Corner Unit—Make 4.

Susan Theobald Fujii
Carson City, Nevada

Every quiltmaker knows how fabric and paraphernalia can sometimes take over the house. In Susan Fujii's case, it has taken over her bedroom and bathroom, permanently.

After more than 12 years of quiltmaking, Sue decided she'd rather have a dyeing room than an extra bathroom. So she and her husband turned the master bathroom and bedroom of their Washoe Valley home into a dyeing space and a sewing room where Sue spends much of her time.

Sue has a strong support group for her quilting. "The quilters in my life are all positive thinkers, creative women who have a wonderful outlook on life," she says. First among these friends is Fran Ulm, whom Sue calls "my partner in quilting." Sue says, "Fran has always encouraged me—everyone should be lucky enough to have a strong influence like her."

"The quilters in my life are all positive thinkers."

Sue is one of a four-woman group, the Buds, who are members of Truckee Meadows Quilters. She also meets twice a month with the QTs, a group that enjoys four-day retreats at least twice a year. Sue is also a member of Creative Quilters of Nevada.

Communion
1999

Classes and workshops give quilters opportunities to learn from each other and share ideas. It was in a class, taught by Robert Callahan, that Susan Fujii discovered this charming block design.

An adaptation of the traditional Tin Man block, the figure represented here might be called "Tin Woman" since she seems to be wearing a dress.

"I loved the warmth and simplicity of this design," says Sue, whose quilts often have a whimsical touch.

She saw the block, or one like it, in a book called *A Communion of the Spirit,* so Sue named her quilt *Communion* because it reminds her of how much friendship and help went into its making—the block idea from Robert and quilting ideas from friends Fran Ulm and Linda Thomas. In many ways, Sue says, "this quilt is about people coming together."

Communion was shown at the 2000 National Quilters Association's Show in Reno.

Communion

Finished Size
Quilt: 67½" x 77½"
Blocks: 42 (6" x 6")

Materials*
⅜ yard *each* 7 fabrics for setting squares and triangles
13 (5" x 15") scraps for dresses
1⅜ yards beige tone-on-tone fabric for block background
1¾ yards brown "flesh" fabric (includes inner border)
⅜ yard check border fabric
2 yards black border fabric (includes binding)
5¼ yards backing fabric
Ivory embroidery floss
42 sets of 3 (¼"-diameter) buttons for dresses (optional; not recommended for children)

* Note: As in all scrap quilts, these yardages are recommendations. Use your own scraps and fabric placement as desired. Add leftover border and setting fabrics to scraps, if desired.

Cutting
Make templates of patterns A, B, C, and F on page 93; J can be rotary cut. Cut pieces in order listed to make best use of yardage. Cut all strips cross-grain.

From each of 6 setting fabrics
- 5 (6½") squares.
- 6 (9¾") squares. Cut each square in quarters diagonally to get 22 side triangles (and 2 extra).

From 7th setting fabric
- 2 (6⅛") squares. Cut each square in half diagonally to get 4 corner triangles. Add remainder of this fabric to dress fabrics.

Machine-quilted by Linda Thomas of Elko, Nevada.

From each dress fabric
- 1 (1" x 15") strip. From this, cut 3 of Template F and 3 of Template F reversed.
- 3 of Pattern C.

From beige fabric
- 5 (2½" x 43") strips. From these, cut 42 (2½") squares. Cut each square in half diagonally to get 84 D triangles.
- 4 (2⅝" x 43") strips. From these, cut 42 of Template A.
- 9 (2¼" x 43") strips. From these and fabric remaining from A strips, cut 84 (2¼" x 4¾") G pieces.

From black fabric
- 4 (6½" x 70") lengthwise strips for borders.

From check fabric
- 7 (1¼" x 43") strips.

From brown fabric
- 4 (2½" x 62") lengthwise strips for inner border.
- 12 (1" x 33") strips. From these, cut 84 (1" x 1½") E pieces, 84 (1") H squares, 42 of Template B, and 42 of Template B reversed.
- 42 (2¼") J squares.

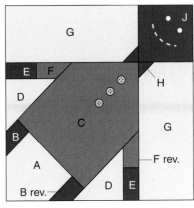

Communion Block—Make 42.

91

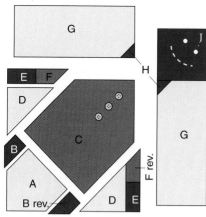

Block Assembly Diagram

Block Assembly

1. Sew Bs and Bs reversed to opposite sides of each A piece (*Block Assembly Diagram*).
2. For 1 block, choose 1 A/B unit, 2 D, 2 E, 2 G, 2 H, and 1 J. Select 1 C, 1 F, and 1 F reversed from same fabric.
3. Sew C to top of A/B unit.
4. Sew Es to straight edges of F and F reversed. Join E/F and E/Fr units to 1 leg of a D triangle as shown. Press seam allowances toward Ds. Sew D/E/F arm units to central dress unit.
5. See page 59 for instructions on Diagonal-Corners Quick-Piecing Method. Use this technique to sew H squares to 1 corner of each G piece. (Note these are mirror-image units; sew corner to upper right corner of 1 G and upper left corner of second G.) Join J square to top of unit with H at upper left corner.
6. Sew G/H to top edge of dress unit. Add G/H/J to right edge. Press seam toward G.
7. Make 42 blocks.
8. Use 4 strands of embroidery floss to make a running stitch smile and French knots for eyes as shown on J pattern (*Stitch Diagrams,* opposite).

Quilt Assembly

1. Lay out blocks, setting triangles, and setting squares in diagonal rows (*Quilt Assembly Diagram*). When satisfied with placement, join blocks and setting pieces in each diagonal row.
2. Add corner triangles.
3. Join rows.

Borders

1. Measure length of quilt top through middle of pieced section. Trim 2 brown border strips to match quilt length. Sew borders to quilt sides, easing to fit.
2. Measure width of quilt top through middle, including side borders. Trim 2 brown borders to match width. Sew borders to top and bottom edges of quilt.
3. Join 2 check strips end-to-end to make each side border. Join 3 remaining check strips end-to-end; then cut long strip in half to get 2 borders for top and bottom edges. Repeat steps 1 and 2 to add middle border.
4. Join black outer border strips to quilt in same manner.

Quilting and Finishing

1. Assemble backing. Layer backing, batting, and quilt top.
2. Outline-quilt patches and add additional quilting as desired.
3. Make 8⅜ yards of straight-grain binding from remaining black fabric. Bind quilt edges.
4. Add buttons as desired.

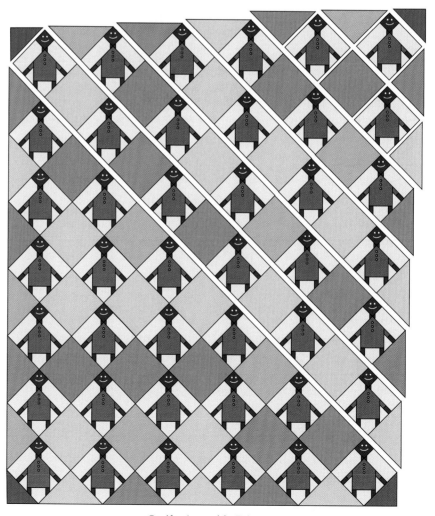

Quilt Assembly Diagram

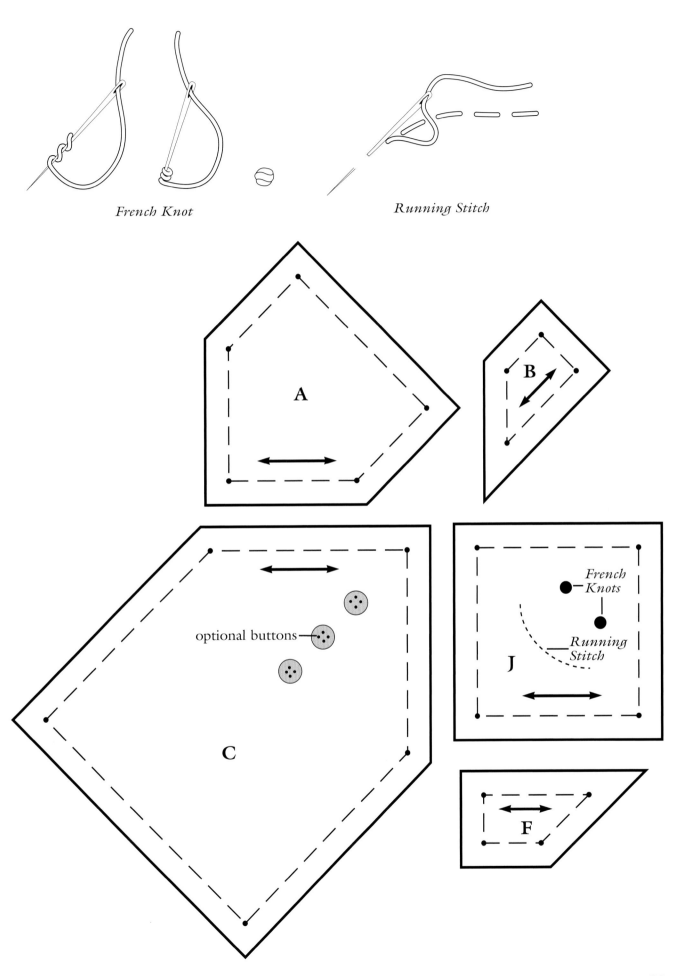

French Knot

Running Stitch

A

B

optional buttons

C

French Knots

Running Stitch

J

F

93

Ruth K. Bates
Bella Vista, Arkansas

Growing up on an Iowa farm during the Depression, Ruth Bates thought quilts were make-shift things patched of feed sacks and scraps of worn-out clothing. "I don't recall ever seeing any quilts as we know them today," she says.

Ruth fell in love with quilts and quilting in 1990 at the Colorado Quilting Council's Quilt Fair in Boulder. Charmed by an appliquéd quilt she saw there, Ruth knew she had to make one. After a lifetime of sewing and tailoring garments, she had the basic skills and she certainly had determination.

"Quilting . . . enables me to make new friends."

When Ruth moved to Arkansas, she joined Bella Vista's Calico Cut-ups Quilt Guild. "I give credit to my guild friends for inspiring and encouraging me," Ruth says.

Quilting and friends are more important to Ruth since her husband passed away. "Quilting is the perfect hobby to fill lonely hours," she says. "It enables me to make new friends, learn new methods, and experiment with original designs."

Ruth is a member of the American Quilter's Society, The Appliqué Society, and Appliqué Artists of Arkansas.

Ohio Rose
1998

It was love at first sight. In 1990, Ruth saw an Ohio Rose quilt at a quilt show in Boulder, Colorado, and she was smitten.

Though she'd never made a quilt before, Ruth confidently bought fabric. She had a pattern for the main block, but drafted her own patterns for the border swags and feather quilting designs. She says, "Had I realized how daunting the task was facing me, I might never have had the courage to start."

Ruth set the work aside for a while when she moved to Arkansas. After she joined a local quilt group, she pulled out the few blocks she'd completed and forged ahead.

That's when she realized she didn't have enough fabric for the appliquéd borders. So she improvised a pillow tuck at the top end of the quilt.

Once the quilt top was complete, Ruth didn't have room to spread it out. But a friend came to the rescue, offering her home for the

basting. After many nights of quilting into the wee hours, Ruth put in the last stitch just days before the guild's 1998 Ozark Quilt Fest. She was thrilled that *Ohio Rose* won Best of Show and Viewers' Choice.

After that success, Ruth's guild friends helped to photograph *Ohio Rose* so she could submit it (successfully) to the jury for the 1999 American Quilter's Society show. "What wonderful friends quilters are," Ruth says.

Ohio Rose

Finished Size

Quilt: 95" x 112½"

Blocks: 13 (17" x 17")

Materials

8¾ yards tan background fabric

3 yards red/green large print fabric

2¾ yards red fabric

2½ yards green small print leaf fabric (includes binding)

¾ yard black solid fabric for stems

3⅜ yards 104"-wide backing

Cutting

Make templates of patterns A–Q on pages 100–104. Cut pieces in order listed to make best use of yardage. Rotary-cut all strips cross-grain. When possible, pieces are listed in order needed, so you don't have to cut everything at once.

From tan fabric

- 1 (88") length. From this, cut 2 (11¾" x 88") strips for side borders.
- 1 (70") length. From this and leftover piece from previous cuts, cut 13 (17½") squares for blocks.
- 1 (51") length. From this, cut 2 (25½") squares. Cut each square in quarters diagonally to get 8 setting triangles. From remainder, cut 2 (13") squares. Cut each square in half diagonally to get 4 corner triangles.
- 1 (96") length. From this, cut 1 (11¾" x 96") strip for bottom border and 1 (29½" x 96") strip for top panel.

Block 1—Make 9.

From red/green large print fabric

- 3 (8"-wide) strips. From these, cut 10 of Pattern E.
- 1 (2¼"-wide) strip. From this, cut 10 of Pattern H.
- 1 (10"-wide) strip. From this, cut 2 of Pattern M and 44 of Pattern C.
- 4 (15"-wide) strips. From these, cut 15 of Pattern P.

From red fabric

- 4 (4"-wide) strips. From these, cut 44 of Pattern D.
- 7 (7"-wide) strips. From these, cut 10 of Pattern F and 15 of Pattern Q.
- 2 of Pattern N.

From green small print fabric

- 6 (6"-wide) strips. From these, cut 38 of Pattern B.
- 2 (6"-wide) strips. From these, cut 22 of Pattern L.
- 4 of Pattern K.

From black fabric

- 3 (3½"-wide) strips. From these, cut 40 of Pattern A.
- 6 (3"-wide) strips. From these, cut 40 of Pattern G and 4 of Pattern J.

Block Assembly

1. For each Block 1, select 4 each of A, B, C, and D, as well as 1 each of E, F, G, H, and a

Block 2—Make 4.

tan background square. Fold square in half vertically, horizontally, and diagonally, making creases for appliqué placement guides *(Diagram A)*. Prepare pieces A–H for appliqué.

2. Pin A and B pieces on diagonal placement lines, with tip of B leaf about 1½" from corner of background square. Center E, covering ends of A stems. Pin Cs and Ds in place. Appliqué A–D in alphabetical order.

3. Center F on E and appliqué. If desired, cut away background and E fabrics from underneath F appliqué, leaving ¼" seam allowances. (This eliminates bulk that may impair quilting.) Center and appliqué G and H pieces.

4. Make 9 of Block 1.

5. Fold remaining 4 background squares in half horizontally and vertically. Align adjacent placement lines with guidelines on

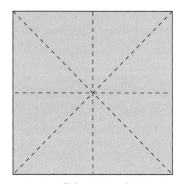

Diagram A

Quilt Assembly Diagram

¼ Wreath Quilting Pattern (page 99); lightly mark design on fabric. Rotate fabric to mark remaining 3 quarters of wreath.

6. Prepare J, K, L, C, and D pieces for appliqué. Center pieces inside wreath on each block. Appliqué J–L in alphabetical order; then stitch C and D in place. Make 4 of Block 2.

Quilt Assembly

1. Lay out blocks in 5 diagonal rows, alternating blocks 1 and 2 as shown *(Quilt Assembly Diagram)*. Place setting triangles at ends of each row.

2. When satisfied with placement, join blocks and triangles in each row. Press seam allowances toward Block 2s and setting triangles. Add corner triangles.

Borders

1. Sew side and bottom borders to edges of quilt. Miter corners. Press seam allowances toward borders.

2. Center M/N swags over each mitered seam; pin. Pin 5 P/Q swags along bottom border between corners. Pin L leaf pieces at juncture of each pair of swags, with leaf tip just touching border seam. Appliqué.

3. Pin 5 P/Q swags along each side border. Pin L pieces in place (last L will extend over end of border; leave it pinned for now, but be sure to keep it out of top border seam line). Appliqué.

Color Variations

This traditional block is adaptable to so many fabric treatments, the sky's the limit. We've created three additional looks that are lovely ideas. Your own fabric stash may suggest even more.

4. Fold top border in half vertically and horizontally to find center. Pin E piece in place at center; then pin A and B pieces on horizontal placement line. Appliqué As and Bs; then position and appliqué Cs and Ds.

5. Trim straight extension from ends of each remaining A stem. Tuck stems under E and pin; then pin remaining Cs and Ds in place. Appliqué.

6. Appliqué E in place. Complete appliqué with F, G, and H.

Trim fabric from behind layered appliqué, if desired.

7. Matching centers, sew top panel to top edge of quilt assembly. Press seam allowances toward top. Complete appliqué of L pieces.

Quilting and Finishing

1. Layer backing, batting, and quilt top.

2. Outline-quilt appliqués. Quilt marked wreath pattern on Block 2s. Pattern for feathers quilted in setting and corner triangles is on page 103. Background area of quilt pictured is quilted in diagonal cross-hatching, with lines spaced 1¼" apart.

3. Make 12 yards of bias or straight-grain binding from remaining green fabric. Bind quilt edges.

Place on fold.

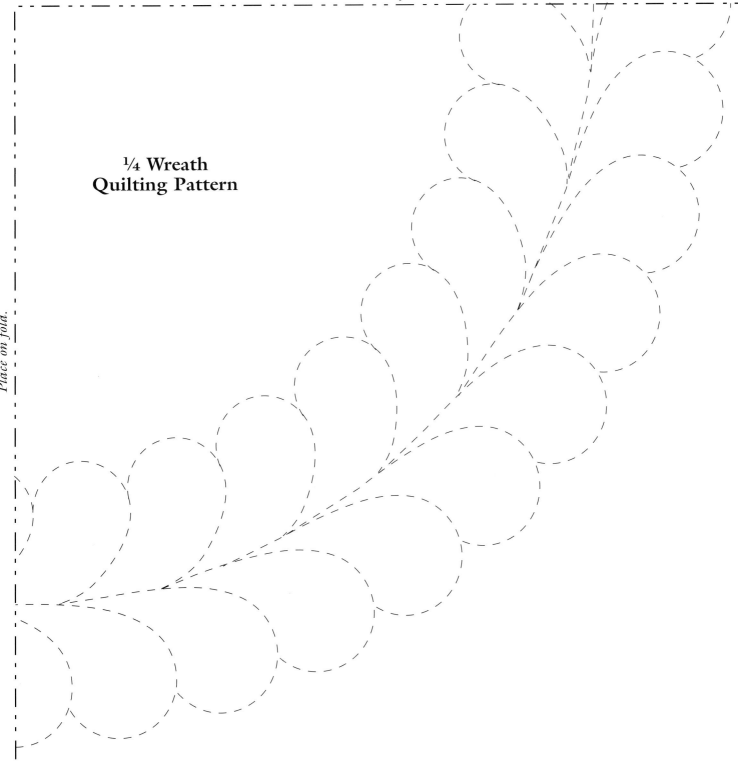

¼ Wreath Quilting Pattern

Place on fold.

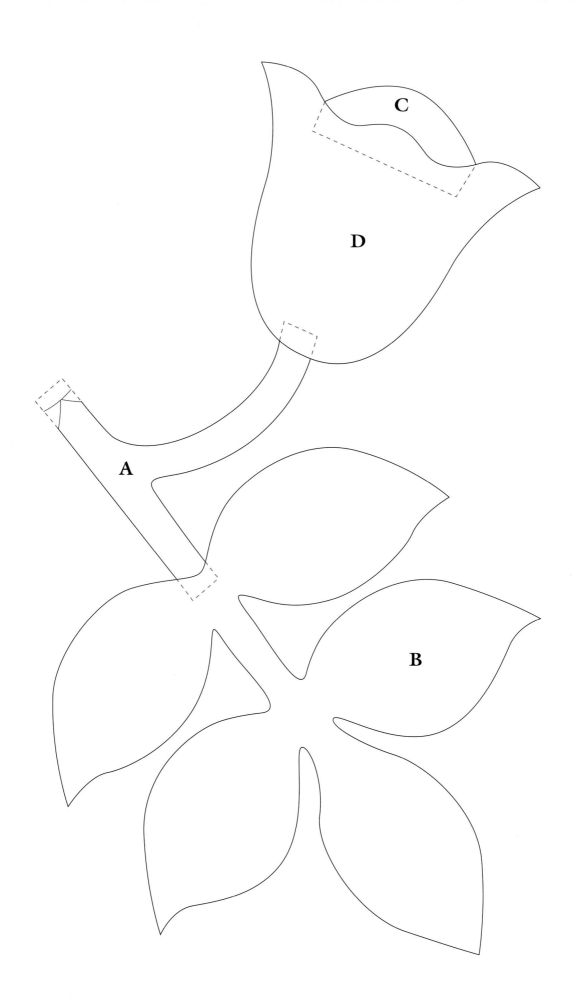

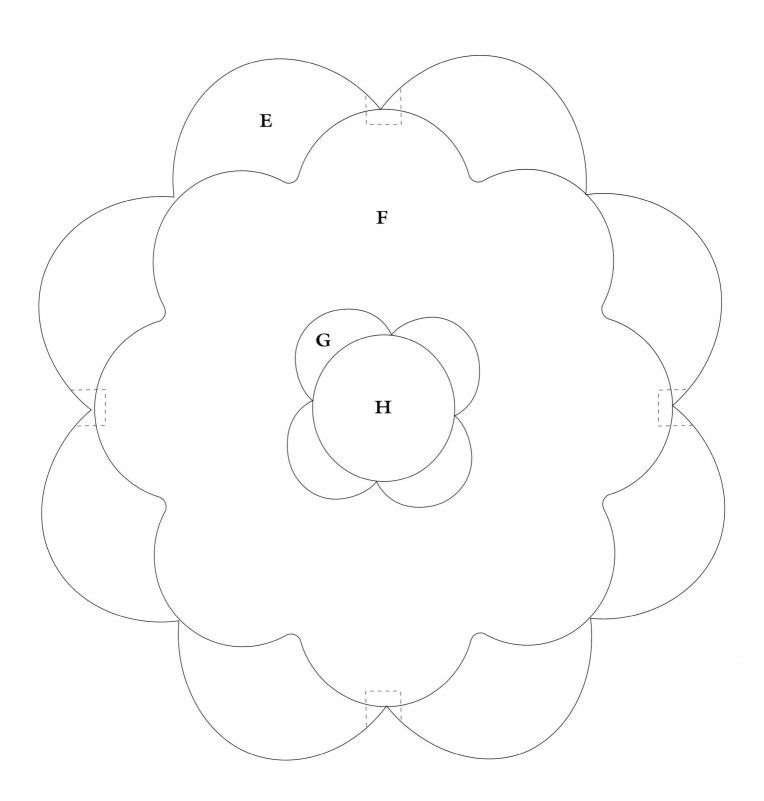

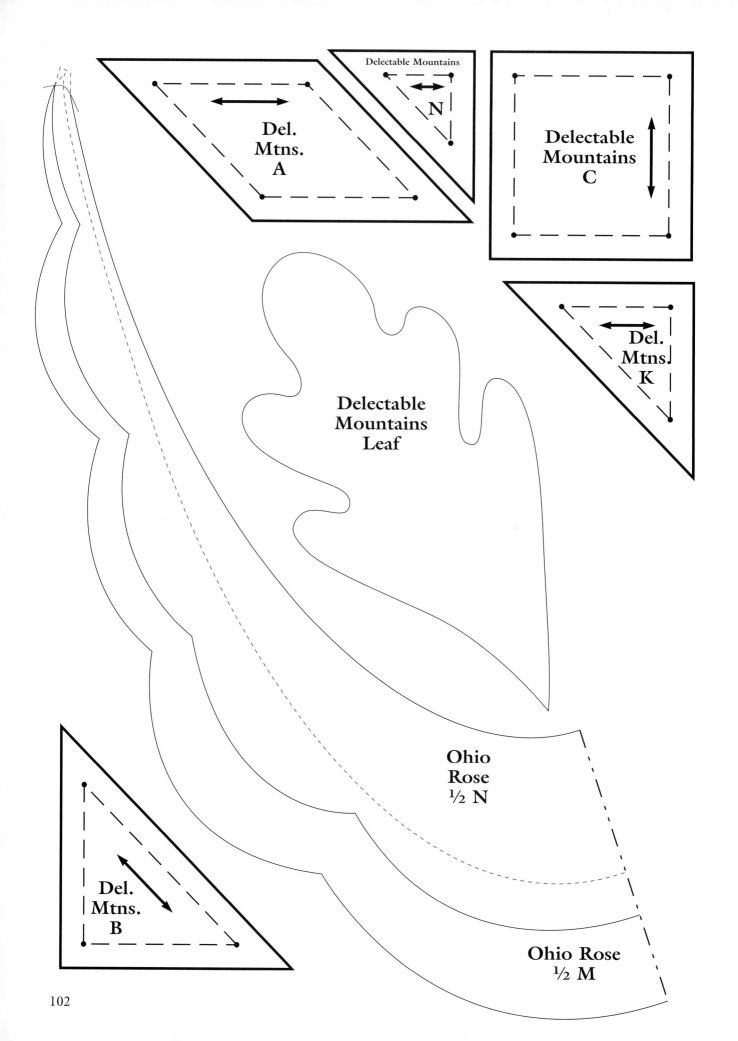

Del.
Mtns.
A

Delectable Mountains

N

Delectable
Mountains
C

Del.
Mtns.
K

Delectable
Mountains
Leaf

Ohio
Rose
½ N

Del.
Mtns.
B

Ohio Rose
½ M

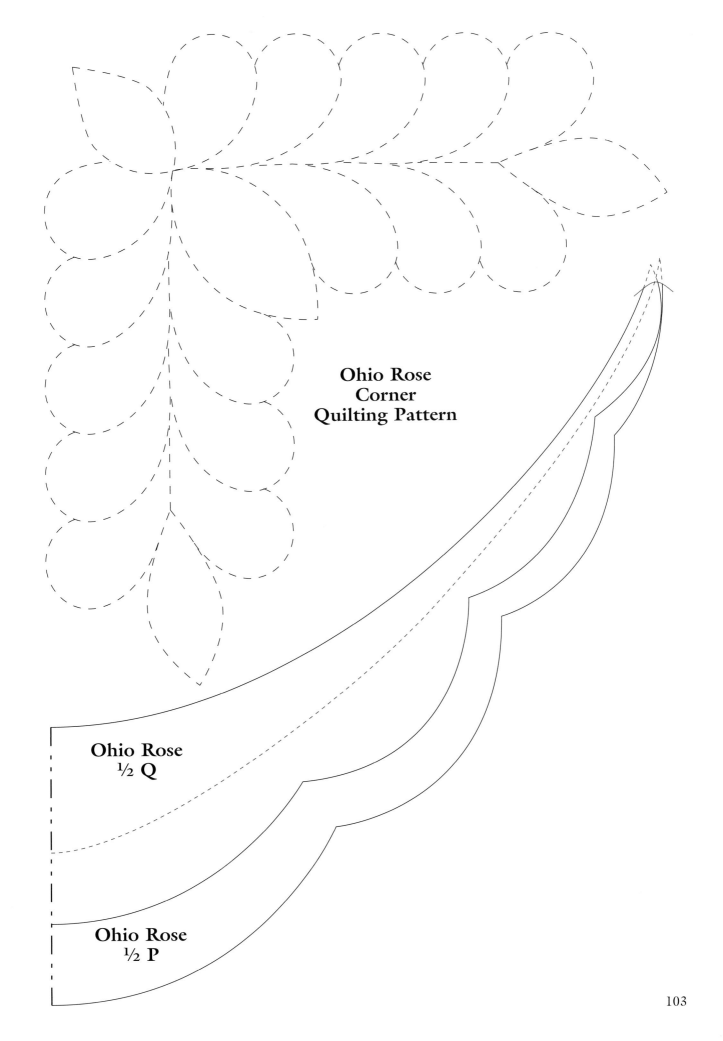

Ohio Rose
Corner
Quilting Pattern

Ohio Rose
½ Q

Ohio Rose
½ P

C

D

L

K

J

Carole Monahan
Gresham, Oregon

Carole Monahan loves that quiltmaking is her link to women of the past, present, and future.

"I'm proud to be a part of the sisterhood of quilters," Carole says, and hopes her quilts will be a legacy like those of her grandmothers and mother before her. "Quiltmaking is an important avenue to connect with women," Carole says. "I love grade-school quilters as much as I do the grandmothers."

A quilter for 25 years, Carole makes quilts both traditional and of original design. She's come a long way since her first wall hanging, in which the Bear's Paw blocks are missing a few toes. With the help of her sister, Eleanor, Carole is now a gifted and "precise" quilter and she teaches at a local quilt shop. Carole tells her students that "heart is an essential ingredient in the making of a quilt."

"Heart is an essential ingredient in the making of a quilt."

Carole is a member of the Skip-a-Week Quilt Guild of Estacada, a group that has held a meeting *every* week since 1921. She is also a member of Lake Oswego's To Bee or Not to Bee and The Book Club, a new group that creates original quilt designs based on books the members read.

Generations
1998

Carole Monahan says that "this is possibly the sweetest quilt I've ever made." And after 25 years of quilting, that's saying a lot.

The 1930s reproduction fabrics that Carole used bring to her mind fond memories of her grandmother's quilts. Because the quilt was made for 4-year-old granddaughter Lauren (who has her own stash of reproduction fabrics for future quilts), Carole feels this quilt spans the generations of her family's quilters.

Carole placed the Square-Within-a-Square blocks on point and defined them with a frame of sashing and cornerstones (sashing squares). The bright borders give the quilt the fresh look she wanted.

Generations was shown at the Pacific Northwest Quilters Show in March 2001.

Generations (Square-Within-a-Square)

Finished Size
Quilt: 75½" x 87½"
Blocks: 50 (7" x 7")

Materials*
50 (4⅜" x 8¾") scrap fabrics
50 (3⅜" x 6¾") scrap fabrics
50 (4½") squares scrap fabrics
2½ yards border fabric (includes binding)
2 yards white print fabric for block centers and sashing
1½ yards blue print setting fabric
5¼ yards backing fabric
* *Note:* As in all scrap quilts, these yardages are recommendations. Use your own scraps and fabric placement as desired. Add leftover border and setting fabrics to scraps, if desired.

Cutting
Cutting and piecing instructions are for rotary cutting and quick piecing. (For traditional piecing, use patterns on page 108.) See tips for diagonal-corners technique, page 59. Cut pieces in order listed to make best use of yardage. Rotary-cut all strips cross-grain. When possible, pieces are listed in order needed, so you don't have to cut everything all at once.
From border fabric
- 4 (4¾" x 82") lengthwise strips for outer border.
- 6 (2" x 24") strips. From these, cut 71 (2") squares for sashing.
- 5 (2½" x 72") lengthwise strips for straight-grain binding.

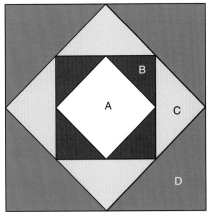

Square-Within-a-Square Block—Make 50.

From white print fabric
- 5 (4"-wide") strips. From these, cut 50 (4") A squares.
- 6 (7½"-wide") strips. From these, cut 120 (2" x 7½") sashing strips.

From blue print setting fabric
- 5 (15¾") squares. Cut each square in quarters diagonally to get 18 setting triangles (and 2 extra).
- 2 (10¼") squares. Cut each square in half diagonally to get 4 corner triangles.

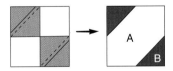

Diagram A

Block Assembly
See Quilt Smart on page 59 for instructions on Diagonal-Corners Quick-Piecing Method.
1. For each block, choose 1 A square and 1 print piece of each size (4½", 3⅜" x 6¾", and 4⅜" x 8¾").
2. Cut 4½" square into 4 (2¼") B squares. Fold each of these squares in half diagonally; crease to mark a sewing line. Use diagonal-corner technique to sew 2 B squares to opposite corners

of A square *(Diagram A)*. Repeat with remaining corners *(Diagram B)*. Press all seam allowances toward B corners.
3. Cut 3⅜" x 6¾" scrap in half to get 2 (3⅜") squares. Cut each square in half diagonally to get 4 C triangles. With right sides facing, align long edge of a triangle with each edge of A/B unit. (Triangle is slightly longer than A/B, so triangle points extend a bit at corners.) Stitch C triangles to each edge of center unit *(Block Diagram)*. Press seam allowances toward Cs.
4. Cut 4⅜" x 8¾" into 2 (4⅜") squares. Cut each square in half diagonally to get 4 D triangles. Sew D triangles to edges of A/B/C unit to complete block. Press seam allowances toward Ds.
5. Make 50 blocks.

Quilt Assembly
1. Lay out blocks in 10 diagonal rows, with sashing strips between blocks *(Quilt Assembly Diagram, page 108)*. Arrange blocks to achieve a pleasing balance of color and pattern.
2. When satisfied with placement of blocks, join blocks and sashing in each diagonal row. Press seam allowances toward sashings.
3. Lay out block rows. Lay out remaining sashing strips and sashing squares in diagonal rows between block rows. Join sashing and squares in each sashing row. (You should have 1 sashing strip

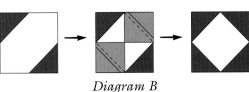

Diagram B

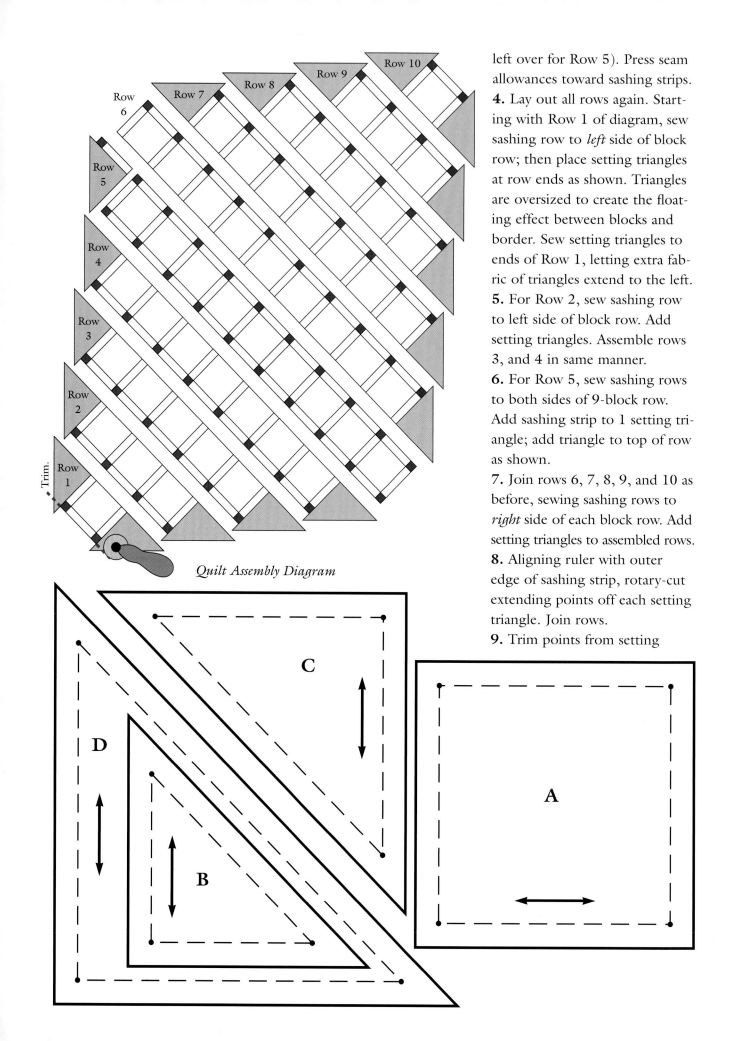

Row 10
Row 9
Row 8
Row 7
Row 6
Row 5
Row 4
Row 3
Row 2
Row 1
Trim.

Quilt Assembly Diagram

left over for Row 5). Press seam allowances toward sashing strips.

4. Lay out all rows again. Starting with Row 1 of diagram, sew sashing row to *left* side of block row; then place setting triangles at row ends as shown. Triangles are oversized to create the floating effect between blocks and border. Sew setting triangles to ends of Row 1, letting extra fabric of triangles extend to the left.

5. For Row 2, sew sashing row to left side of block row. Add setting triangles. Assemble rows 3, and 4 in same manner.

6. For Row 5, sew sashing rows to both sides of 9-block row. Add sashing strip to 1 setting triangle; add triangle to top of row as shown.

7. Join rows 6, 7, 8, 9, and 10 as before, sewing sashing rows to *right* side of each block row. Add setting triangles to assembled rows.

8. Aligning ruler with outer edge of sashing strip, rotary-cut extending points off each setting triangle. Join rows.

9. Trim points from setting

C

D

B

A

Machine-quilted by Janet Fogg.

triangles on rows 1 and 10. Add corner triangles. Press seam allowances toward triangles.

Borders

1. Measure length of quilt top through middle of pieced section. Trim 2 border strips to match quilt length.

2. Sew borders to quilt sides, easing to fit as needed. Press seam allowances toward borders.

3. Measure width of quilt top through middle, including side borders. Trim remaining borders to match width. Sew borders to top and bottom edges of quilt, easing to fit as needed. Press.

Quilting and Finishing

1. Assemble backing. Layer backing, batting, and quilt top.

2. Quilt as desired. Quilt shown is machine-quilted in an allover swirl pattern.

3. Make 9¼ yards of straight-grain binding from reserved strips. Bind quilt edges.

Tish Fiet
Jackson, Mississippi

*I*n May of 1993, when Tish Fiet asked a friend to teach her to quilt, Tish made it clear that she didn't want to join any quilting groups, take classes, or attend shows. By the end of that summer, Tish had joined a quilting group, taken a class, attended several quilt shows, and was trying to complete her quilt in time to enter it in a show. "Obviously, I was hooked," Tish says.

That first quilt, a Drunkard's Path pattern from *Great American Quilts 1991*, was juried into the American Quilter's Society's

"Sewing machines stress me out."

1994 show and she has shown three more quilts in Paducah since then (she won an Honorable Mention ribbon in 2000).

All of Tish's quilts are stitched by hand. "Sewing machines stress me out," she says with a laugh. A love of fabric is evident in her many scrap quilts and the large closet in which her extensive fabric collection is stored, neatly organized by color and pattern.

A former accountant, Tish retired in 1999 and now spends 30 to 35 hours a week on her quilting, with the goal of making an heirloom quilt for each family member. She enjoys floral appliqué to combine quilting with her other love, gardening and flowers,

Tish is a member of a small local group, Quilters Square. She is also a member of the American Quilter's Society.

That's Cool
1999

When Tish Fiet's grandson, Hunter, saw the quilt she had made for him, he exclaimed, "That's cool!"

Hunter, who often accompanies Tish to quilt shows, selected the colors and the Winding Ways pattern for his quilt, and Tish used a window-style template to cut the pieces from about 60 different fabrics.

That's Cool won a first-place ribbon at the Pine Belt Quilters' show in Hattiesburg, Mississippi, in 1999. It was also shown at the 1999 Quilters Heritage Celebration in Lancaster, Pennsylvania.

That's Cool

Finished Size
Quilt: 66" x 79"
Blocks: 99 (5¾" x 5¾")

Materials*
17 (18" x 22") fat quarters light
  scrap fabrics
17 (18" x 22") fat quarters dark
  scrap fabrics
⅝ yard turquoise accent fabric
3 yards border fabric (includes
  binding)
4 yards backing fabric
Note: As in all scrap quilts,
yardages are recommendations.
Use your own scraps as desired.
Using leftover border fabrics in
blocks will reduce the number of
scrap fabrics needed.

Cutting
Make templates of patterns X, Y,
and Z on page 114. Use a ¹⁄₁₆"-
diameter hole punch to punch
out corner dots on each template. Cut pieces in order listed
to make best use of yardage.
From light fabrics
• 49 sets of 4 Y pieces.
• 50 sets of 4 X pieces and 4 Z
  pieces.
From dark fabrics
• 50 sets of 4 Y pieces.
• 49 sets of 4 X pieces and 4 Z
  pieces.
From turquoise accent fabric
• 8 (1½"-wide) cross-grain
  strips for inner border.
• 7 (1"-wide) cross-grain strips
  for binding accent flange.
From border fabric
• 4 (6¼" x 68") lengthwise
  strips.
• 1 (32") square for binding.

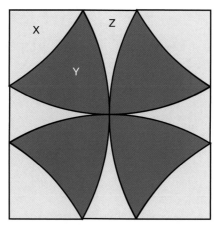

Winding Ways Block 1—Make 50.

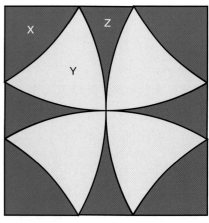

Winding Ways Block 2—Make 49.

Block Assembly
1. For each Block 1, choose 1
set of dark Y pieces and matching sets of light X and Z pieces.
2. See Quilt Smart on page 27
for tips on sewing a curved
seam. Piece curved X/Y seams to
make 4 corner units (*Block
Assembly Diagram*). Press seam
allowances toward Bs.
3. Sew a Z piece to 1 side of 1
corner unit; then join another
corner unit to opposite side of Z
to make a half block as shown.
Press seam allowances toward Ys.

Hole Punch Source
It's not easy to find a single-
hole punch that's as small as
you'd like for marking templates. Some office-supply
stores carry similar products,
but the holes tend to be larger than we need. For a nice
¹⁄₁₆"-diameter hole punch,
here's a mail-order source.
Ask for Product #3271-01.

Family Treasures
24922 Anza Drive, Unit A
Valencia, CA 91355
(800) 413-2645

4. Sew Zs to both sides of 1
remaining corner unit. Press.
Sew remaining Z to last corner
unit as shown. Join both corner
units to make second half-block.
5. Carefully sew curved seam to
join block halves. Press.
6. Make 50 of Block 1. Use light
Y pieces and dark X and Z pieces
to make 49 of Block 2 in same
manner.

Quilt Assembly
1. Referring to photo, lay out
blocks in 11 horizontal rows
with 9 blocks in each row. Start
Row 1 (and all odd-numbered
rows) with a Block 1 and alternate blocks 1 and 2 across row.

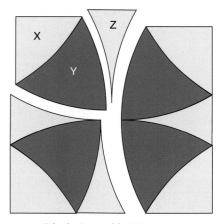

Block Assembly Diagram

Start Row 2 (and all even-numbered rows) with a Block 2 and alternate blocks across row.
2. When satisifed with placement of blocks, join blocks in each row. Press all joining seam allowances toward Block 2s. Then join rows.

Borders
1. Join 2 accent fabric strips end-to-end to make a border strip for each side of quilt.
2. Measure length of quilt top through middle of pieced section. Trim 2 border strips to match quilt length. Sew borders to quilt sides, easing to fit as

needed. Press seam allowances toward borders.
3. Measure width of quilt top through middle, including side borders. Trim remaining borders to match width. Sew borders to top and bottom edges of quilt, easing to fit as needed. Press seam allowances toward borders.

4. Repeat steps 2 and 3 to join outer borders to quilt.

5. Join 2 flange strips end-to-end. Press pieced strip in half lengthwise, wrong sides facing. Matching raw edges, baste strip to outer border along 1 side of quilt. Repeat for opposite side.

For top and bottom edges, piece remaining flange strips to fit. Fold and press each strip; then baste to quilt edges.

Quilting and Finishing

1. Assemble backing. Layer backing, batting, and quilt top.

Backing seams will be parallel to top and bottom edges of quilt.

2. Quilt as desired. Quilt shown is outline-quilted.

3. Make 8⅛ yards of bias or straight-grain binding from reserved fabric. Bind quilt edges.

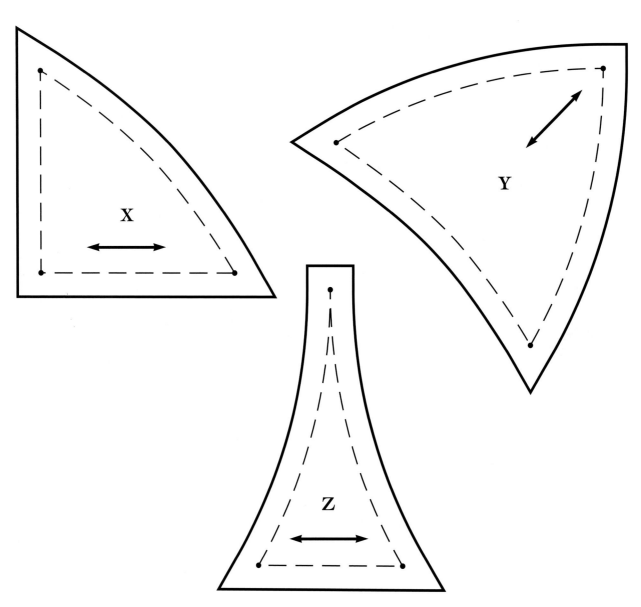

Color Variations

If cool's not your thing, you can make a Winding Ways quilt that's hot stuff using bright, warm colors. Or take a softer approach with pastels. Do your own thing—that's cool, too.

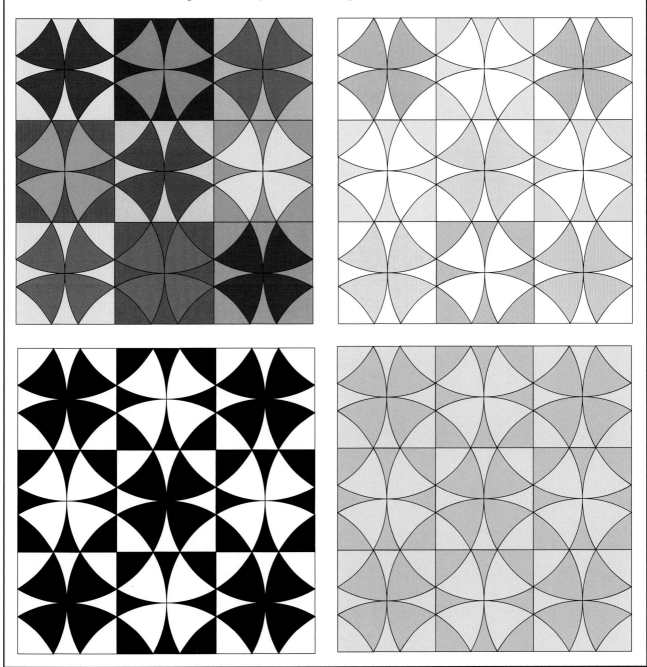

Lorraine Swann
Mount Airy, Maryland

Quilting is a family affair for Lorraine Swann. She made her first quilt, a Log Cabin, more than 40 years ago under the supervision of an aunt. Today, with more than 20 quilts to her credit, Lorraine often quilts with her sister. But most of all, she treasures the quilting time she shares as teacher to her granddaughter and great granddaughter.

Lorraine belongs to a seven-woman quilting bee, quilts once a week at a local church, and works on fundraising quilts at the Mount Airy Senior Center. "I enjoy the friendships I've found in my quilting groups," Lorraine says. "We all enjoy going to quilt shows together."

Delectable Mountains
1998

This quilt is an interpretation of a classic 1850s design. The muslin and navy fabrics are reminiscent of the indigo prints so popular during the mid-nineteenth century.

Delectable Mountains is one of the earliest American patterns, named for a site in John Bunyan's 1678 *Pilgrim's Progress*. A favorite allegory of early settlers, the story chronicles the travels of Christian, a pilgrim, and his quest for the Celestial City.

After much trial and tribulation, Christian at last comes to the Delectable Mountains, a peaceful land of lovely gardens and orchards within sight of the Celestial City.

Lorraine's *Delectable Mountains* won a second-place ribbon at Quilt Odyssey 2000 in Gettysburg, Pennsylvania. It was also shown at Quilters Heritage Celebration, Lancaster, Pennsylvania, in 1999.

Delectable Mountains

Finished Size
Quilt: 88" x 88"
Blocks: 5 (20" x 20")

Materials
7 yards navy print fabric
   (includes binding)
6½ yards muslin
3 yards 104"-wide backing fabric

Cutting
Make templates of patterns A, B, C, K, N, and Leaf on page 102; other pieces can be rotary cut.

Cut pieces in order listed to make best use of yardage. When possible, pieces are listed in order needed, so you don't have to cut everything all at once. However, we recommend cutting largest and/or longest pieces first; then cut smaller pieces as needed. Rotary-cut all strips cross-grain except as noted.

From navy print fabric
- 1 (70") length. From this, cut:
  - 4 (3⅜" x 70") lengthwise strips for inner border.
  - 2 (2½" x 70") lengthwise strips for sashing.
  - 9 (4⅞" x 24½") strips. From these, cut 44 (4⅞") squares. Cut each square in half diagonally to get 88 D triangles.
  - 64 of Pattern A.
- 8 (8½"-wide) strips. From these, cut 40 (8½") squares for F triangle-square grids.
- 1 (68") length. From this, cut:
  - 2 (34") squares. Set aside for border vine bias and for binding.
  - 18 (1⅞" x 9") strips. From this, cut 72 (1⅞") squares. Cut each square in half diagonally to get 144 F triangles.
  - 2 (2½" x 26") corner sashing strips.
- 4 (2½"-wide) strips. From these, cut 8 (2½" x 20½") sashing strips.
- 4 (5¼") squares. Cut each square in quarters diagonally to get 16 L triangles.
- 16 of Pattern N.
- 5 (3½"-wide) strips. From these, cut 40 of Leaf Pattern.

From muslin
- 1 (90") length. From this, cut:
  - 2 (8½" x 90") and 2 (8½" x 72") lengthwise border strips. Add remaining fabric to next cut.
- 6 (8½"-wide) strips. From these and fabric remaining from borders, cut 40 (8½") squares for F triangle-square grids.
- 1 (2¾"-wide) strip. From this, cut 24 of Pattern B.
- 2 (2½"-wide) strips. From these, cut 32 of Pattern C.
- 2 (3¼"-wide) strips. From these, cut 18 (3¼") squares. Cut each square in quarters diagonally to get 72 E triangles.

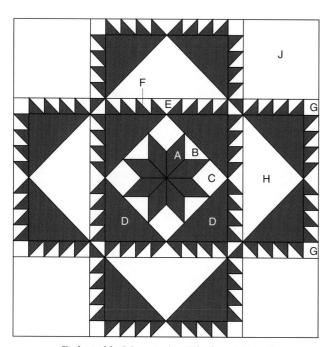

Delectable Mountains Block —Make 5.

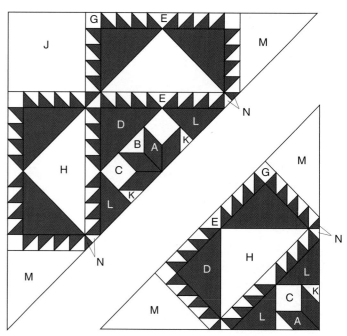

Half-Block—
Make 4.

Corner-Block—Make 4.

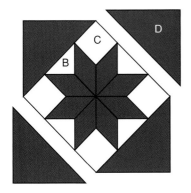

Diagram A

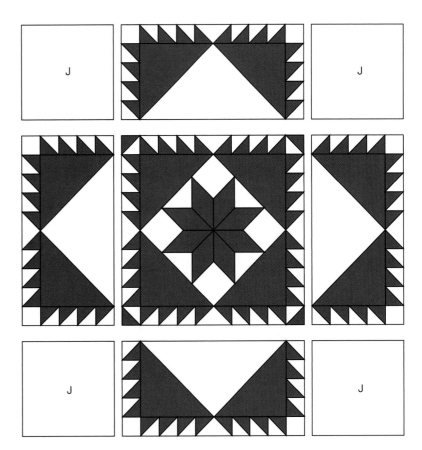

Block Assembly Diagram

Diagram B

- 3 (1½"-wide) strips. From these, cut 72 (1½") G squares.
- 3 (6½"-wide) strips. From these, cut 16 (6½") squares. Cut each square in half diagonally to get 32 H triangles.
- 3 (5½"-wide) strips. From these, cut 24 (5½") J squares. (If fabric is not a full 44" wide, use scrap from previous cut to cut last 3 squares.)
- 1 (8⅜"-wide) strip. From this, cut 4 (8⅜") squares. Cut each square in quarters diagonally to get 16 M triangles.
- 16 of Pattern K.
- 16 of Pattern N.

Block Assembly

1. See Quilt Smart on page 120 for instructions on assembling eight-pointed star. Use A, B, and C pieces to make 1 star unit.

2. Sew D triangles to opposite sides of star *(Diagram A)*. Press seam allowances toward Ds. Sew D triangles to remaining sides of star; press. Set aside.

3. For triangle-squares, use 8½" squares of navy and muslin. On wrong side of a muslin square, draw a 4-square by 4-square grid of 1⅞" squares *(Grid Diagram)*,

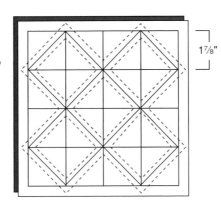

Grid Diagram

leaving a ½" margin on all sides of grid. Draw diagonal lines through squares as shown.

4. Match marked muslin square with a navy square, right sides facing. Sew a ¼" seam on both sides of all diagonal lines. (Blue lines on diagram indicate inside paths; red line indicates outside path.) Leave needle down in fabric to pivot at corners. Press. Stitch 3 grids for each block.

5. Cut on all drawn lines to get 32 triangle-squares from each grid (84 triangle-squares for 1 block; set 12 extras aside for half-blocks). Press triangle-square seam allowances toward navy.

6. Sew 2 navy F triangles to both short legs of a muslin E triangle. Make 8 E/F units for each block. Press seam allowances toward Es.

119

❖QUILT SMART❖
Machine-Stitching an Eight-Pointed Star with Set-In Seams

To sew an eight-pointed star with sharp points and nicely inset corners, don't stitch across the seam allowance as in most patchwork. Use this technique to set the pieces together.

With a fine-tipped marker or pencil, lightly mark seam lines on the *wrong* side of each fabric piece to define the crucial matching point. (In diagrams, this point is indicated by a black dot.)

1. With right sides facing, match 1 diamond to short leg of 1 triangle *(Diagram 1)*. With triangle on top, begin at ¼" seam line. Sew 2 stitches forward and 2 stitches back, taking care not to stitch into the seam allowance. (Arrows indicate stitching direction.) Stitch to edge of fabric (no need to backstitch here because another seam will cross and hold this seam in place). Clip thread and take work out of sewing machine.

2. With right sides facing, match another diamond to second short leg of triangle. With triangle on top, sew from outside edge to inner match point and backstitch *(Diagram 2)*.

3. With right sides facing, match points and edges of diamonds. Fold triangle out of the way. Beginning at inner match point, sew to edge of fabric *(Diagram 3)*.

4. Press center seam open and triangle's seam allowances toward diamonds *(Diagram 4)*. Trim "ears" of seam allowances even with unit edges. This is Unit 1 of the star. Make 4 of Unit 1.

5. To make Unit 2, add a square to right edge of Unit 1. With right sides facing and square on top, start at inner match point and sew to outer edge *(Diagram 5)*. Press seam allowances toward diamonds. Make 4 of Unit 2.

6. Select 2 of Unit 2 for each Unit 3. With right sides facing, match square of 1 Unit 2 to diamond of second Unit 2 *(Diagram 6)*. With square on top, stitch from outside edge, ending with a backstitch at inner seam line.

7. With right sides facing, align unstitched edges of diamonds, folding other pieces out of the way. Pin-match diamonds; then add more pins so you

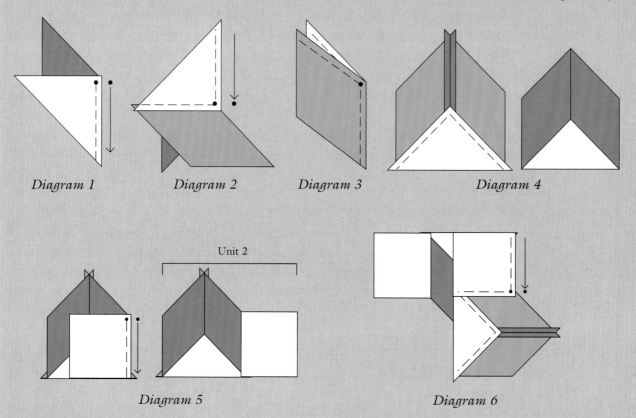

Diagram 1   *Diagram 2*   *Diagram 3*   *Diagram 4*

Unit 2

Diagram 5   *Diagram 6*

can remove positioning pin. Begin sewing with a backstitch at inner seam line *(Diagram 7)* and stitch through Unit 1 seams to edge of fabric. Press diamond seams open and corner-square seams toward center of block. Make 2 of Unit 3 *(Diagram 8)*.

8. To join Unit 3, sew squares to diamonds as described in Step 4.

9. With right sides facing, use a positioning pin to match diamonds at center. Pin seam and remove positioning pin before sewing *(Diagram 9)*. Backstitch at top seam line and stitch precisely through center, ending with a backstitch at seam line. Press seam allowance open. Press corner seam allowances toward diamonds *(Diagram 10)*.

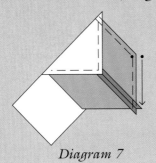

Diagram 7

Unit 3

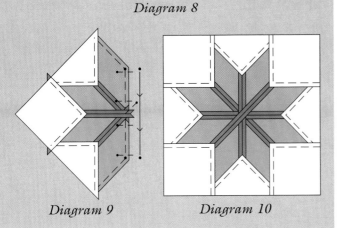

Diagram 8

Diagram 9   *Diagram 10*

7. For center star unit, select 28 triangle-squares and 4 E/F units. Sew 3 triangle-squares on both ends of each E/F, positioning navy triangles to match E/F *(Diagram B)*. Press. Sew 2 rows to opposite sides of star. Press seam allowances toward Ds. Add corner triangle-squares to 2 remaining rows, positioning triangles as shown. Sew rows to remaining sides of star to complete center unit.

8. For side unit, sew D triangles to short legs of an H triangle *(Side Unit Diagram)*. Press seam allowances toward Ds. Add a row of 6 triangle-squares and an E/F to top edge. Then join 4 more triangle-squares in a row, adding a G square at 1 end as shown. Sew to side edge of unit. Repeat on opposite side. Press seam allowances toward Ds. Make 4 side units for each block.

9. Lay out center star unit and 4 side units in rows, adding J squares at each corner as shown *(Block Assembly Diagram)*. Join units in rows; then join rows to complete block.

10. Make 5 blocks.

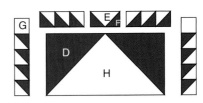

Side Unit Diagram

Partial-Block Assembly

Refer to *Half-Block Diagram* and *Corner Block Diagram* (page 118) throughout.

1. For half-block, use 4 As, 1 B, 2 Cs, and 2 Ks to make 1 half star. Add D and L triangles as shown. Press seam allowances toward triangles. Set aside.

2. Stitch 2 triangle-square grids to get 41 triangle-squares for 1 block; set 23 extras aside (or use extras when you have enough). Press triangle-square seam allowances toward navy.

3. Sew navy F triangles to both short legs of an E triangle. Make 4 E/F units for each half-block. Press seam allowances toward Es.

4. For center star unit, select 13 triangle-squares and 2 E/F units. On both ends of each E/F, sew 3 triangle-squares. Sew 1 row to 1 side of star. Join 2 N triangles as shown and add that triangle to end of sewn triangle-square row. Press seam

121

Quilt Assembly Diagram

allowances toward D. Add corner triangle-square to remaining row, positioning triangles as shown. Sew row to remaining side of star; then add another pair of N triangles to end of row to complete center unit.

5. Make 2 side units.

6. Lay out center star unit and side units in rows. Add J square at corner and M triangles at row ends. Join units in rows; then join rows to complete half-block.

7. Make 4 half-blocks.

8. Make corner block in same manner, using A, C and K pieces to make star unit. Sew L triangles to unit sides as shown. Add row of 1 E/F and 6 triangle-squares to 1 side of star unit; then add pairs of N triangles at row ends. Make 1 side unit; join

this to star unit. Complete corner block with 2 M triangles. Make 4 corner blocks.

Quilt Assembly

1. Setting corner blocks aside for now, lay out whole blocks and half-blocks in 3 diagonal rows *(Quilt Assembly Diagram)*. Place 20½" sashing strips between blocks. Join blocks and sashing strips in each row. Press seam allowances toward sashing.

2. Sew sashing strips and corner blocks to ends of middle row.

3. Sew 70"-long sashing strips to sides of middle row. Press seam allowances toward sashing. Trim ends of sashing even with outside edge of corner blocks.

4. Join remaining rows to both sides of middle row.

5. Sew 26" sashing to long edge of each remaining corner block. Trim excess fabric from ends of sashing even with sides of corner block. Add to quilt corners.

Borders

1. Measure length of quilt top through middle of pieced section. Trim 2 inner border strips to match quilt length. Sew borders to quilt sides, easing to fit as needed. Press seam allowances toward borders.

2. Measure width of quilt top through middle, including side borders. Trim remaining inner border strips to match width. Stitch borders to top and bottom edges of quilt, easing to fit as needed. Press.

3. Mark center on edge of each inner border.

4. For sawtooth border, make 4 E/F units and stitch 9 triangle-square grids to get 264 F triangle-squares (and 24 extra). For each border, join 33 triangle-squares on either side of center E/F unit, positioning navy triangles to match those in E/F.

5. Matching centers and ends, sew 2 sawtooth borders to opposite sides of quilt, easing to fit as needed. Press seam allowances toward inner border.

6. Sew G squares to ends of each remaining sawtooth border. Sew borders to remaining quilt sides, easing to fit as needed.

7. See page 144 for tips on making continuous bias. Use navy 34" square to make 14½ yards of 2"-wide bias for border vine.

8. Referring to photo, center and pin vine on each muslin

border strip in gentle, undulating curves. Prepare leaves for appliqué and pin in place as shown. When satisfied with placement, complete appliqué.

9. Sew shorter borders to top and bottom edges; then sew longer borders to sides. Press seam allowances toward muslin borders.

10. For sawtooth border, make 4 E/F units and stitch 10 grids to get 320 triangle-squares (you

need 336 for outer border; you should have 16 left over from previous grids). For each border, join 42 triangle-squares on either side of E/F unit.

11. Matching centers and ends, sew 2 borders to opposite sides of quilt, easing to fit as needed. Press seam allowances toward muslin borders. Add G squares to 2 leftover borders and sew these to remaining quilt sides.

Quilting and Finishing

1. Layer backing, batting, and quilt top.

2. Quilt as desired. Quilt shown is outline-quilted; feather motifs from commercial stencils are quilted along vine, in H and M triangles, and in J squares.

3. Make 10 yards of straight-grain or bias binding from navy square. Bind quilt edges.

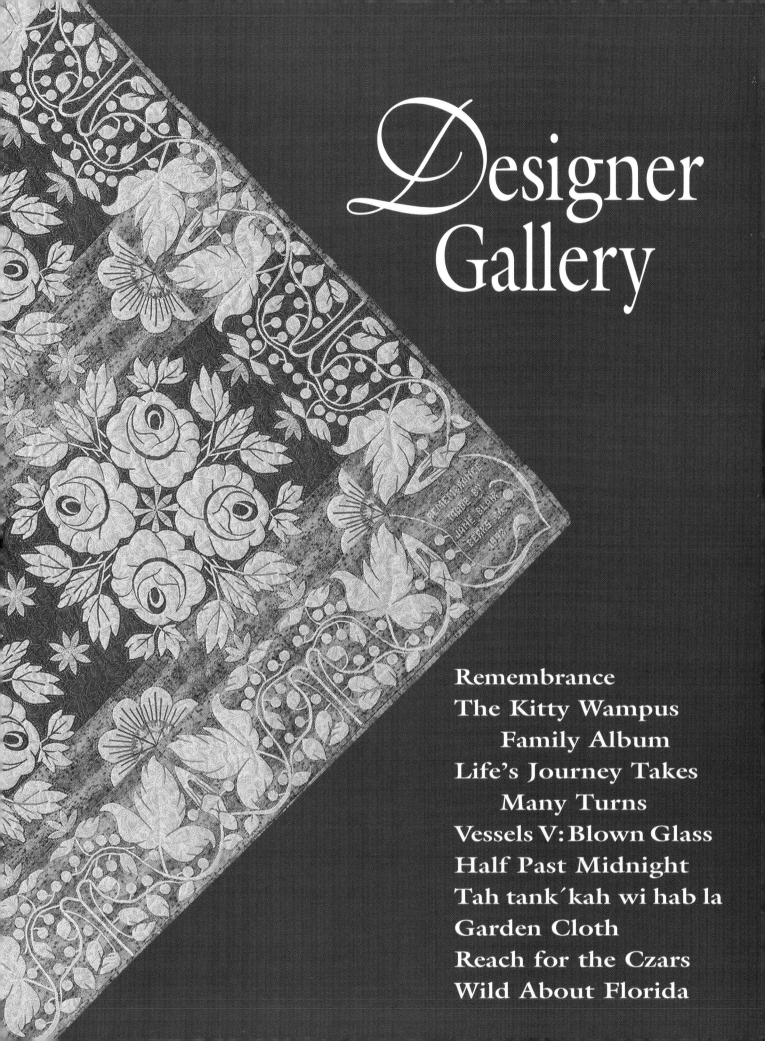

Designer Gallery

Jane Blair
Wyomissing, Pennsylvania

According to the saying, everything old is new again. That's what happens when Jane Blair designs a quilt.

"My work begins with the quilt blocks created and named by quilters of the past," Jane says. Using color, fabric, and design, she discovers new design possibilties in traditional patterns. Innovative design is well and good, Jane says, but she strives for results that are "more pleasing to the eye than shocking to the soul." She considers her work a success when it seems traditional to some and contemporary to others; she says, "The blending of old and new is my goal."

"The blending of old and new is my goal."

Jane is often asked to define how she designs. She says inspiration can come from anything. "Maybe it's instinct," she says. "The clicks of a creative mind shouldn't be over-analyzed. To assign each line and color a reason destroys the illusion."

Few quilters have earned higher accolades. Jane's quilts are exhibited world-wide and hang in national museums. Her numerous awards include Best of Show at the American Quilter's Society show in 1988. That quilt, *Gypsy in My Soul,* was named one of the 20th century's 100 best quilts by an international jury.

Jane is a member of the National Quilting Association, the International Quilt Association, The American Quilter's Society, the National Museum of Women in the Arts, and a lifetime Honorary member of The Pennsylvania Quilters.

Remembrance
1998, 70" x 72"

Browsing through Safford and Bishop's *America's Quilts & Coverlets* one day, Jane Blair spotted a small but intriguing black and white photo of an antique woven coverlet.

Jane worked out a pattern that had a similar look and feeling. "I insist on originality in my quilts," she says.

The design began as a drawing from which Jane made templates. The appliqué is needle-turned, and all the embroidery is machine sewn except for a cross-stitch label in the lower right corner (see enlarged photo on page 125).

The elements in the quilt seem to be perfect, but Jane says there are differences in flowers, leaves, and elements of embroidery. "I eye-balled much of the design," she says. "I don't seek perfection; I aim for the total effect."

Remembrance was Pennsylvania's finalist at the American Quilter's Society's 2000 Quilt Exposition in Nashville.

Rosellen Carolan
Auburn, Washington

Remember the good old days? Rosellen Carolan recalls making her first quilt in the mid-1970s. A Boston Commons design made from dress scraps, she marked, cut, and sewed each square one by one. Today she can laugh and say, "Where were the rotary cutter and speed-piecing techniques then?"

"Never be afraid to ask a fellow quilter for help. Quilters are the most generous and sharing people I know."

Rosy's quilts remained traditional through the 1980s as her quiltmaking skills improved. The '90s brought new ideas and new techniques; she began keeping an "inspiration box" of photos, cards, and other things that gave her ideas for new quilts. "I see things now with an artist's eye," she says. "I'm always thinking about how to turn an image into a quilt."

Anyone can be creative, Rosellen says, "if we give ourselves time to experiment, learn, and practice, practice, practice." Every quilt doesn't have to be a masterpiece, she says. "Learning by trial and error is an important part of the process." Most of Rosellen's current pieces are contemporary machine work, but she also finds time to hand-quilt her collection of antique tops.

Rosellen is a member of the Evergreen Piecemakers Quilt Guild, the Contemporary Quilt Art Association, and the Association of Pacific Northwest Quilters.

128

The Kitty Wampus Family Album
1999, 70" x 77"

Rosellen Carolan has had a lifetime of feline friends, including Spike, the orange tom who currently rules her home. So when she found a wrapping paper that showed cats doing "people" things, she knew it had to be a quilt. "I always suspected cats don't spend *all* their time sleeping," she says. "They imitate us when we're not looking."

Using ideas from the wrapping paper and some of her own, Rosellen started making blocks. "Like all the cats I've had, each block has its own personality," she says. With Grandpa in the tub, aunties dressed for church, and bachelor Tom in his hot-rod, a family was born. (Rosellen says this clan is descended from pioneer barn cats.) And

no family album is complete without a group photo. After setting the blocks out of kilter, or "catty-wampus," the play-on-words title emerged.

The Kitty Wampus Family Album has won ribbons at the Western Washington State Fair, Evergreen Piecemakers Quilt Show, and the 2000 International Quilt Association show in Houston, Texas.

Peggy Waltman
Sandy, Utah

*J*ust when something precious is lost, something else may be found. Life is funny that way. So when Peggy Waltman's health began to decline, she found quilting.

Quiltmaking came into Peggy's life at about the same time that she was diagnosed with an autoimmune disease. Encouraged by a neigh-bor to try quilting, Peggy was thrilled by the fabrics and colors—they seemed to provide some of the energy that illness had stolen from her.

"Quilting has become the voice of my spirit and my soul."

Like many beginners, Peggy started out following patterns and making traditional quilts. More than seven years later, now she tries something new with every project. She says that since she's been sick, "quilting has become the voice of my spirt and my soul."

Peggy thinks of her quilts as part of her legacy to her eight children. She says, "With my quilts, I'll leave a part of myself with my family forever."

When you're doing something special, word gets around. "People were call-ing me out of the blue, wanting to come see my quilts," Peggy says. She got so many requests for patterns of her original designs, Peggy formed a company called Hopskotch to sell them. In 2001, Hopskotch published a book of Peggy's quilts entitled *Hope and Cheer.* (You can contact Peggy about her book by e-mail at hopskotchquiltingco@hotmail.com.)

Peggy is a member of the Utah Quilt Guild.

Life's Journey Takes Many Turns
2000, 48" x 48"

Peggy Waltman started this quilt with a New York Beauty paper-piecing pattern by Karen Stone. Then, Peggy says, "I went crazy on my own."

Though some of the 16 fan units are similar, no two are quite alike. Peggy used a scrappy palette of red, gold,

and green to diversify the blocks, adding appliquéd circles for embellishment. The wavy outer path is a lot like the ups and downs of life.

Life's Journey Takes Many Turns won an Honorable Mention at the 2000 Pacifiic International Quilt Festival.

Robbi Joy Eklow
Grayslake, Illinois

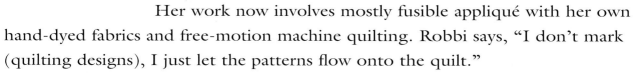

*R*obbi Joy Eklow went to college to study engineering. But her love of textiles won out in the end. A quiltmaker she had to be.

After a lifetime of sewing, beading, and playing with fabric, Robbi started quilting in earnest in 1987 when she joined a quilt guild and began taking workshops. Soon she discovered that she wasn't limited to geometric pieced images. "I realized I could fuse anything I could draw," she says.

"I just let the patterns flow onto the quilt."

Her work now involves mostly fusible appliqué with her own hand-dyed fabrics and free-motion machine quilting. Robbi says, "I don't mark (quilting designs), I just let the patterns flow onto the quilt."

Robbie is concentrating on two on-going series of quilts. In the still lifes, she adds a bit of surrealism to images of everyday housewares such as vases, cups, bowls, and teapots. Her puzzle quilts are in a cubist-like style.

Some of the best things in Robbi's life come through quilting—great friends, travel opportunities, and many awards for her work. She lectures and teaches for guilds around the country. Robbi is a member of Illinois Quilter's, Inc.

Vessels V: Blown Glass
1998, 54" x 72"

Robbi Eklow was making quilts like this for a while before she realized she was working in a cubist style. This quilt was shown at the Quilter's Heritage Celebration in 2000 and won the Best Use of Color Award at the 1999 Mid-Atlantic Quilt Festival.

Half Past Midnight
2000, 63" x 63"

This quilt is Robbi's homage to the new millenium. When she created the design, she says, "I imagined I'd been to a New Year's party, wearing pearls and drinking from a beautiful wine glass. But the party's over and I'm getting ready to go to sleep."

Robbi's design places ordinary objects in a colorful dream-like setting, blending elements of real and unreal.

In addition to dyeing the fabrics, Robbi fuses the pieces in place and uses extensive free-motion machine quilting to embellish the design.

Half Past Midnight won a ribbon for machine quilting at the 2000 International Quilting Association show. It was also exhibited at the Mid-Atlantic Quilt Festival and the American Quilter's Society shows in 2000.

Jean Ann Williams
Sun City, Arizona

*Y*ears ago, Jean Ann Williams was cleaning out her mother-in-law's home when she found an old suitcase in the back of a closet. Inside was a quilt, an 1890s red and white Federal Chain.

"I sometimes try to imagine the woman who made it," Jean says. "Who was she?" That quilt led Jean to decide to make quilts for every member of her family. She says, "I hope my quilts will last as long as the one I found, and that they will be treasured as a gift from my heart through my hands."

"I've met the best of friends in quilting groups."

Quiltmaking is a serious hobby for Jean, who likes to keep her hands busy in the evening. She became involved in quilting when she joined the Blue Ridge Quilter's Guild of Johnson City, Tennessee. That's when she started to attend shows, take classes, and concentrate on improving her skills. "My husband's job took us to several states," Jean explains. "Each time we moved, I'd unpack one week, and the next week I'd join the local guild. I've met the best of friends in quilting groups."

Jean is a member of the Arizona Quilter's Guild and the National Quilter's Association, as well as a past member of groups in Tennessee and Florida.

Tah tank´ kah wi hab la (Bison Dreams)
1998, 78½" x 80"

Jean Williams' husband, Troy, has a passion for southwest heritage, history, and native wildlife. So, when Jean made this quilt for him, she chose its name from the Oglala Sioux language.

The design is worked in reverse appliqué on a whole cloth. Jean says, "The best part about reverse appliqué was that I needed only black thread."

Jean's original designs represent the bison, fish, coyote, desert tortoise, jackrabbit, Gila monster, and tarantula.

The graduated gray hoof prints that walk across the quilt top are the real shape of bison prints. At the center edges, a Saguaro cactus is silhouetted against a night sky and the morning sun.

Jean had a gray fabic in mind, but Troy chose the

black background fabric. "I thought I'd go blind trying to quilt on black," Jean says, "but I chose a gray quilting thread that turned out to be easy to see." The quilting is an adaptation of an Apache basketry design.

Jean's quilt was Best of Show at the 1998 Arizona State Fair. It was shown at the 2000 National Quilter's Association show in Reno, Nevada.

134

Rebecca Chapin
Fountain, Colorado

*F*amilies that relocate often know how difficult it can be to make friends in a new town. But quiltmakers like Rebecca Chapin know where to find kindred spirits.

"Quilting has always provided me with instant connections and friends," she says. That was important to Rebecca when she was a young mother who needed an adult outlet.

"I love trying new things."

The friends and creative satisfaction she found in quilting "kept my brain from turning into oatmeal," she jokes.

When Rebecca started quilting 20 years ago, she machine-pieced baby quilts for her children. "I worked into hand appliqué as my children got older and I had more time," she says

Becky was 2001 president of Colorado Springs Piecing Partners Quilt Guild.

Garden Cloth
1999, 82" x 82"

This lavishly appliquéd quilt was inspired by a photograph Rebecca saw of a nineteenth-century embroidered tablecloth made in Australia.

She selected an elegant tone-on-tone beige print for the background and worked the lattice and greenery in blue and green to provide a cool setting for brilliant red tulips.

Garden Cloth was juried into the American Quilter's Association's 2000 show in Paducah, Kentucky.

Reach for the Czars
1998, 81" x 83"

"I see quilt designs all around me," Rebecca Chapin says. She took bits of inspiration from different sources and combined them to make this brightly colored quilt.

The design is based on a photograph of a Russian brocade scarf woven in the early 1900s. The sweeping feathers and plumes are reminiscent of the Russian imperial crest of a crowned two-headed eagle with outstretched wings.

Rebecca was inspired to select the colors for the quilt by a cloisonné tea set of Russian make.

Reach for the Czars was awarded a third-place ribbon in the Amateur Appliqué category at the 1998 American Quilter's Association show in Paducah, Kentucky. It also was judged Best of Show in the Fine Arts Division at the 1998 Colorado State Fair.

Venice Area Quilters Guild
Venice, Florida

*I*n the Gulf Coast communities around Venice, more than 100 "snowbirds" join local quiltmakers to swell the ranks of the Venice Area Quilters Guild. "More than half of us live part of the year somewhere else, mostly up North,"

"We bring ideas from many different places."

says guild member Janet Aronson. During the cold weather months, these quiltmakers enjoy the Florida sunshine as well as day-long workshops and programs with nationally known speakers at least six times a year.

Annual challenges, monthly block contests, and small group get-togethers keep the needles busy in Venice. The members also make quilts for a local pregnancy-care center and for children with cancer. Members are always on hand for events with the Sarasota Alliance for the Arts and other local programs.

The 2000 raffle quilt, *Wild About Florida,* raised $8,000 for the Venice guild. The proceeds are dedicated to guild programs and retreats, as well as local charities.

Wild About Florida
2000, 95" x 101"

The raffle quilt for the Venice Area Quilters Guild's 2000 show had to be something worthy of commemorating a new millenium. It was a goal fulfilled by more than 50 group members.

Janet Aronson and Judy Egan designed 16 original appliqué blocks celebrating Florida's natural treasures. Each block features an animal and flowers such as hibiscus, lilies, and fuschia. The feathered and furry natives include a pelican, armadillo, manatee, and alligator.

A team of five selected fabrics for the quilt; then 16 women each began stitching a block. Once the quilt top was assembled, stitchers added gulls, terns, and sandpipers. Others took on the hand-quilting, stitching many of the same flower and tree motifs in the blocks. The guild's letters "VAQG" and "2000" are quilted in the border.

Wild About Florida was juried into the American Quilter's Association 2000 show in Paducah, Kentucky.

QUILT SMART WORKSHOP
A Guide to Quiltmaking

Preparing Fabric

Before cutting any pieces, be sure to wash and dry your fabric to preshrink it. All-cotton fabrics may need pressing before cutting. Trim selvages from the fabric before you cut pieces.

Making Templates

Before you can make one of the quilts in this book, you must make templates from the printed patterns given. (Not all pieces require patterns—some pieces are meant to be cut with a rotary cutter and ruler.) Quilters have used many materials to make templates, including cardboard and sandpaper. Transparent template plastic, available at craft supply and quilt shops, is durable, see-through, and easy to use.

To make a plastic template, place the plastic sheet on the printed page and use a laundry marker or permanent fine-tip marking pen to trace each pattern. For machine piecing, trace on the outside solid (cutting) line. For hand piecing, trace on the inside broken (stitching) line. Cut out the template on the traced line. Label each template with the pattern name, letter, grain line arrow, and match points (corner dots).

Marking and Cutting Fabric for Piecing

Place the template facedown on the wrong side of the fabric and mark around it with a sharp pencil.

If you will be piecing by machine, the pencil lines represent cutting lines. Cut on each marked line.

For hand piecing, the pencil lines are seam lines. Leave at least ¾" between marked lines for seam allowances. Add ¼" seam allowance around each piece as you cut. Mark match points (corner dots) on each piece.

You can do without templates if you use a rotary cutter and ruler to cut straight strips and geometric shapes such as squares and triangles. Rotary cutting is always paired with machine piecing, and pieces are cut with seam allowances included.

Hand Piecing

To hand piece, place two fabric pieces together with right sides facing. Insert a pin in each match point of the top piece. Stick the pin through both pieces and check to be sure that it pierces the match point on the bottom piece (*Figure 1*). Adjust the pieces as necessary to align the match points. (The raw edges of the two pieces may not align exactly.) Pin the pieces securely together.

Sew with a running stitch of 8 to 10 stitches per inch. Sew from match point to match point, checking the stitching as you go to be sure you are sewing in the seam line of both pieces.

To make sharp corners, begin and end the stitching exactly at the match point; do not stitch into the seam allowances. When joining units where several seams come together, do not sew over seam allowances; sew through them at the point where all seam lines meet (*Figure 2*).

Always press both seam allowances to one side. Pressing the seam open, as in dressmaking, can leave gaps between stitches through which the batting may beard. Press seam allowances toward the darker fabric whenever you can, but it is sometimes more important to reduce bulk by avoiding overlapping seam allowances. When four or more seams meet at one point, such as at the corner of a block, press all the seams in a "swirl" in the same direction to reduce bulk (*Figure 3*).

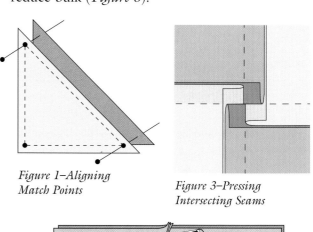

Figure 1–Aligning Match Points

Figure 3–Pressing Intersecting Seams

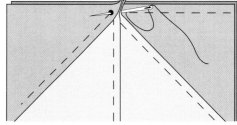

Figure 2–Joining Units

Machine Piecing

To machine piece, place two fabric pieces together with right sides facing. Align match points as described under "Hand Piecing" and pin the pieces together securely.

Set the stitch length at 12 to 15 stitches per inch. At this setting, you do not need to backstitch to lock seam beginnings and ends. Use a presser foot that gives a perfect ¼" seam allowance, or measure ¼" from the needle and mark that point on the presser foot with nail polish or masking tape.

Chain piecing, stitching edge to edge, saves time when sewing similar sets of pieces (*Figure 4*). Join the first two pieces as usual. At the end of the seam, do not backstitch, cut the thread, or lift the presser foot. Instead, sew a few stitches off the fabric. Place the next two pieces and continue stitching. Keep sewing until all the sets are joined. Then cut the sets apart.

Press seam allowances toward the darker fabric whenever possible. When you join blocks or rows, press the seam allowances of the top row in one direction and the seam allowances of the bottom row in the opposite direction to help ensure that the seams will lie flat (*Figure 5*).

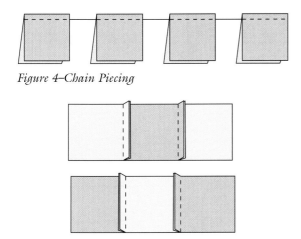

Figure 4–Chain Piecing

Figure 5–Pressing Seams for Machine Piecing

Hand Appliqué

Hand appliqué is the best way to achieve the look of traditional appliqué. But using freezer paper, which is sold in grocery stores, saves time because it eliminates the need for hand basting seam allowances.

Make templates without seam allowances. Trace the template onto the *dull* side of the freezer paper; cut the paper on the marked line. Make a freezer-paper shape for each piece to be appliquéd.

Pin the freezer-paper shape, *shiny side up*, to the *wrong side* of the fabric. Following the paper shape and adding a scant ¼" seam allowance, cut out the fabric piece. Do not remove the pins. Use the tip of a hot, dry iron to press the seam allowance to the shiny side of the freezer paper. Be careful not to touch the shiny side of the freezer paper with the iron. Remove the pins.

Pin the appliqué shape in place on the background fabric. Use one strand of sewing thread in a color to match the appliqué shape. Using a very small slipstitch (*Figure 6*) or blindstitch (*Figure 7*), appliqué the shape to the background fabric.

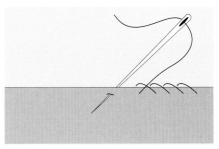

Figure 6–Slipstitch

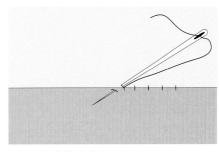

Figure 7–Blindstitch

When your stitching is complete, cut away the background fabric behind the appliqué, leaving ¼" seam allowance. Separate the freezer paper from the fabric with your fingernail and pull gently to remove it.

Mitering Borders

Mitered borders take a little extra care to stitch but offer a nice finish when square border corners just won't do.

First, measure the length of the quilt through the middle of the quilt top. Cut two border strips to fit this length, plus the width of the border plus 2". Centering the measurement on the strip, place pins on the edge of each strip at the center and each end of the measurement. Match the pins on each border strip to the corners of a long side of the quilt.

Starting and stopping ¼" from each corner of the quilt, sew the borders to the quilt, easing the quilt to fit between the pins (*Figure 8*). Press seam allowances toward border strip.

Measure the quilt width through the middle and cut two border strips to fit, adding the border width plus 2". Join these borders to opposite ends of the quilt in the same manner.

Fold one border corner over the adjacent corner (*Figure 9*) and press. On the wrong side, stitch in the creased fold to stitch a mitered seam (*Figure 10*). Press; then check to make sure the corner lies flat on the quilt top. Trim seam allowances.

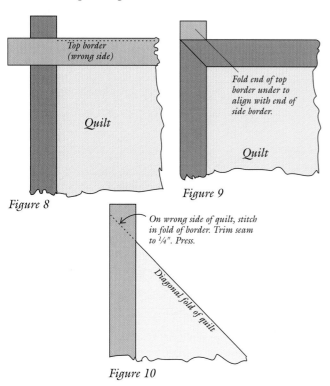

Figure 8

Figure 9

Figure 10

Mitering Borders

Marking Your Quilt Top

When the quilt top is complete, press it thoroughly before marking it with quilting designs. The most popular methods for marking use stencils or templates. Both can be purchased, or you can make your own. You can also use a yardstick to mark straight lines or grids.

Use a silver quilter's pencil for marking light to medium fabrics and a white chalk pencil on dark fabrics. Lightly mark the quilt top with your chosen quilting designs.

Making a Backing

The instructions in *Great American Quilts* give backing yardage based on 45"-wide fabric unless a 90"-wide or 108"-wide backing is more practical. (These fabrics are sold at fabric and quilt shops.) Pieced or not, the quilt backing should be at least 3" larger on all sides than the quilt top.

Backing fabric should be of a type and color that is compatible with the quilt top. Percale sheets are not recommended, because they are tightly woven and difficult to hand-quilt through.

A pieced backing for a bed quilt should have three panels. The three-panel backing is recommended because it tends to wear better and lie flatter than the two-panel type, the center seam of which often makes a ridge down the center of the quilt. Begin by cutting the fabric in half widthwise (*Figure 11*). Open the two lengths and stack them, with right sides facing and selvages aligned. Stitch along both selvage edges to create a tube of fabric (*Figure 12*). Cut down the center of the top layer of fabric *only* and open the fabric flat (*Figure 13*). Press seam allowances toward center panel.

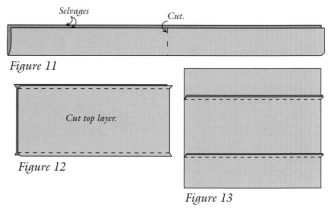

Figure 11

Figure 12

Figure 13

Making a Three-Panel Backing

Layering and Basting

Prepare a working surface to spread out the quilt. Place the backing on the surface, right side down. Unfold the batting and place it on top of the backing. Smooth any wrinkles or lumps in the batting. Lay the quilt top right side up on top of the batting and backing. Make sure backing and quilt top are parallel.

Use a darning needle for basting, with a long strand of sewing thread. Begin in the center of your quilt and baste out toward the edges. The stitches should cover enough of the quilt to keep the layers from shifting during quilting. Inadequate basting can result in puckers and folds on the back and front of the quilt during quilting.

Hand Quilting

Hand quilting can be done with the quilt in a hoop or in a floor frame. It is best to start in the middle of your quilt and quilt out toward the edges.

Most quilters use a thin, short needle called a "between." Betweens are available in sizes 7 to 12, with 7 being the longest and 12 the shortest. If you are a beginning quilter, try a size 7 or 8. Because betweens are so much shorter than other needles, they may feel awkward at first. As your skill increases, try using a smaller needle to help you make smaller stitches.

Quilting thread, heavier and stronger than sewing thread, is available in a wide variety of colors. If color matching is critical and you can't find the color you need, you can substitute cotton sewing thread if you coat it with beeswax before quilting to prevent it from tangling.

Thread your needle with a 20" length and make a small knot at one end. Insert the needle into the quilt top approximately ½" from the point where you want to begin quilting. Do not take the needle through all three layers, but stop it in the batting and bring it up through the quilt top again at your starting point. Tug gently on the thread to pop the knot through the quilt top into the batting. This anchors the thread without an unsightly knot showing on the back.

With your non-sewing hand underneath the quilt, insert the needle with the point straight down in the quilt about 1/16" from the starting point. With your underneath finger, feel for the point as the needle comes through the backing (*Figure 14*). Place the thumb of your sewing hand approximately ½" ahead of the needle. When you feel the needle touch your underneath finger, push the fabric up from below as you rock the needle down to a nearly horizontal position. Using the thumb of your sewing hand in conjunction with the underneath hand, pinch a little hill in the fabric and push the tip of the needle back through the quilt top (*Figure 15*).

Now either push the needle all the way through to complete one stitch or rock the needle again to

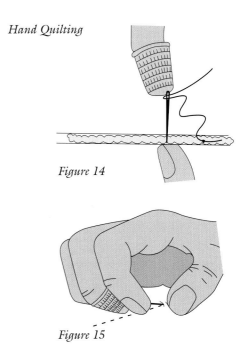

Hand Quilting

Figure 14

Figure 15

an upright position on its point to take another stitch. Take no more than a quarter-needleful of stitches before pulling the needle through.

When you have 6" of thread remaining, you must end the old thread securely and invisibly. Carefully tie a knot in the thread, flat against the surface of the fabric. Pop the knot through the top as you did when beginning the line of quilting. Clip the thread, rethread your needle, and continue quilting.

Machine Quilting

Machine quilting is as old as the sewing machine itself; but until recently, it was thought inferior to hand quilting. Fine machine quilting is an exclusive category, but it requires a different set of skills from hand quilting.

Machine quilting can be done on your sewing machine using a straight stitch and a special presser foot. A walking foot or even-feed foot is recommended for straight-line quilting to help the top fabric move through the machine at the same rate that the feed dogs move the bottom fabric.

Regular sewing thread or nylon thread can be used for machine quilting. With the quilt top facing you, roll the long edges of the basted quilt toward the center, leaving a 12"-wide area unrolled in the center. Secure the roll with bicycle clips, metal bands that are available at quilt shops. Begin at one unrolled end and fold the quilt over and over until only a small area is showing. This will be the area where you will begin to quilt.

Place the folded portion of the quilt in your lap. Start quilting in the center and work to the right, unfolding and unrolling the quilt as you go. Remove the quilt from the machine, turn it, and reinsert it in the machine to stitch the left side. A table placed behind your sewing machine will help support the quilt as it is stitched.

Curves and circles are most easily made by free-motion machine quilting. Using a darning foot and with the feed dogs down, move the quilt under the needle with your fingertips. Place your hands on the fabric on each side of the foot and run the machine at a steady, medium speed. The length of the stitches is determined by the rate of speed at which you move fabric through the machine. Do not rotate the quilt; rather, move it from side to side as needed. Always stop with the needle down to keep the quilt from shifting.

Making Binding

A continuous bias or straight-grain strip is used to bind quilt edges. Bias binding is especially recommended for quilts with curved edges. Follow these steps to make a continuous bias strip:

1. Start with a square of fabric. Multiply the number of binding inches needed by the cut width of the binding strip (usually 2½"). Use a calculator to find the square root of that number. That's the size of the fabric square needed to make your binding.
2. Cut the square in half diagonally.
3. With right sides facing, join triangles to form a sawtooth as shown (*Figure 16*).
4. Press seam open. Mark off parallel lines the desired width of the binding as shown (*Figure 17*).
5. With right sides facing, align raw edges marked Seam 2. Offset edges by one strip width, so one side is higher than the other (*Figure 18*). Stitch Seam 2. Press seam open.
6. Cut the binding in a continuous strip, starting with the protruding point and following the marked lines around the tube.
7. Press the binding strip in half lengthwise, with wrong sides facing.

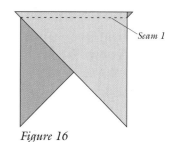

Figure 16

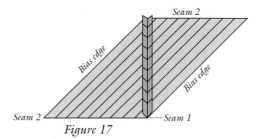

Figure 17

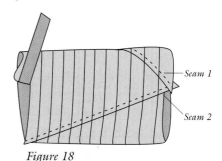

Figure 18

Continuous Bias Binding

Attaching Binding

To prepare your quilt for binding, baste the layers together ¼" from the edge of the quilt. Trim the backing and batting even with the edge of the quilt top. Beginning at the midpoint of one side of the quilt, pin the binding to the top, with right sides facing and raw edges aligned.

Machine-stitch the binding along one edge of the quilt, sewing through all layers. Backstitch at the beginning of the seam to lock the stitching.

Stitch until you reach the seam line at the corner, and backstitch. Lift the presser foot and turn the quilt to align the foot with the next edge. Continue sewing around all four sides. Join the beginning and end of the binding strip by machine, or stitch one end by hand to overlap the other.

Turn the binding over the edge and blindstitch it in place on the backing. At each corner, fold the excess binding neatly to make a mitered corner and blindstitch it in place.